By Karol Ann Krakauer

Picture Songs 1A
for beginning pianists

Picture Songs Classical 1B

Picture Songs 1C

Picture Songs 2
Scales - Chords - Fingering -Timing
& Other Music Theory
to be studied along with book 3 & 4

Picture Songs 3
Songs of God and Country

Picture Songs 4
More Songs of God and Country

Picture Songs 5
Songs From Around the World
with bilingual lyrics

Picture Songs 6
Spanish Songs
with bilingual lyrics

PICTURE SONGS 6
SONGS FROM AROUND THE WORLD
with bilingual lyrics

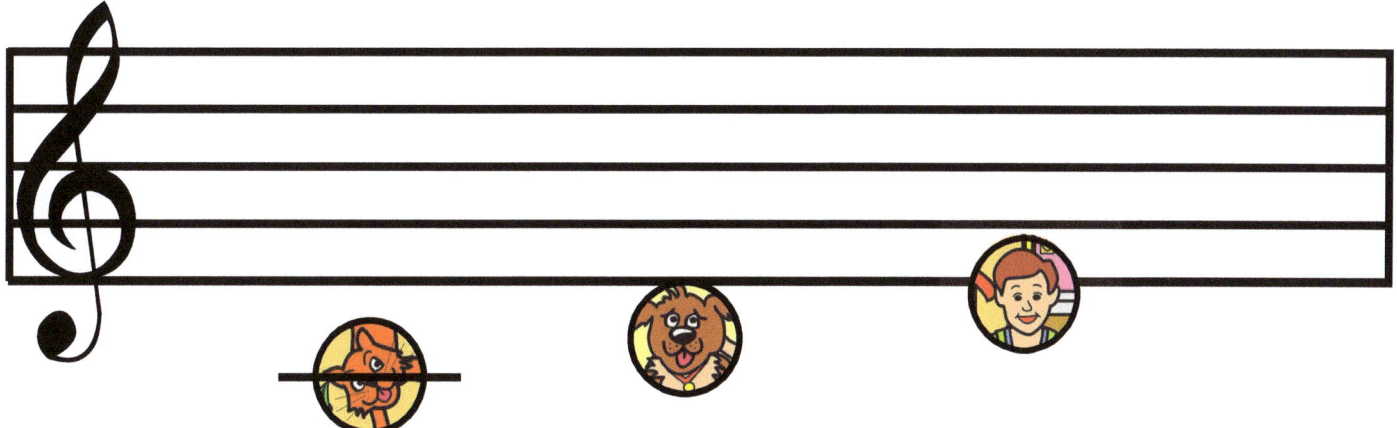

by Karol Ann Krakauer
Fort Collins, Colorado
2018

COPYRIGHT © 2018
by Karol Ann Krakauer
available at Amazon.com

Illustrations copyright 2004 by Evans-Perucca

All rights reserved. No part of this book may be reproduced or transmitted in any form or by any means, electronic or mechanical, without the permission of the publisher.

First Edition

picturesongs@outlook.com
picturesongsonline.com

To Jason and his siblings, Heidi, Amanda and Garrett, who started the whole thing.

Table of Contents

Introduction		8
Chord Review		9
Counting Review		10
French Songs:	French Numbers	12
	Days of the Week	13
	Frere Jacques	14
	Alouette	16
Spanish Songs:	La Cucaracha	18
	Las Mañanitas	20
Swedish Song:	Troll Mom's Lullaby	22
German Song:	Brahms Lullaby	28

Introduction

As you progress with your piano skills, you will be building on what you have learned in Picture Songs Books 1A - 1B - 1C - 2 - 3 - 4 and 5 Spanish Songs. Review your counting, chording and music theory so you will be ready to use it here.

Many of you are learning languages as well. This book and Picture Songs 5 Spanish Songs were written to combine your music and singing skills with language learning. I have included songs from a few countries you may know. The lyrics include the foreign language, the pronounciation when available and the English translation.

Our dear friend, Armelle, from Brittany, France was kind enough to provide the French pronunciation and translation.

We are fortunate to have had Mary Daline, a Spanish teacher, provide the Spanish pronounciation and translation.

Maria, our painter, from Sweden, sang the Troll Mom's Lullaby to us in our garage while sitting on Michael's motorcycle. We fell in love with it immediately and had to include it. Fortunately we found the composer, and she graciously gave us permission to use her sweet song.

Seraina Gessler was kind enough to provide the German pronunciation.

If you send me a public domain language song that I end up using in a future book, I will send you a free book of your choice from my series. Send to: picturesongs@outlook.com.

Chord Review

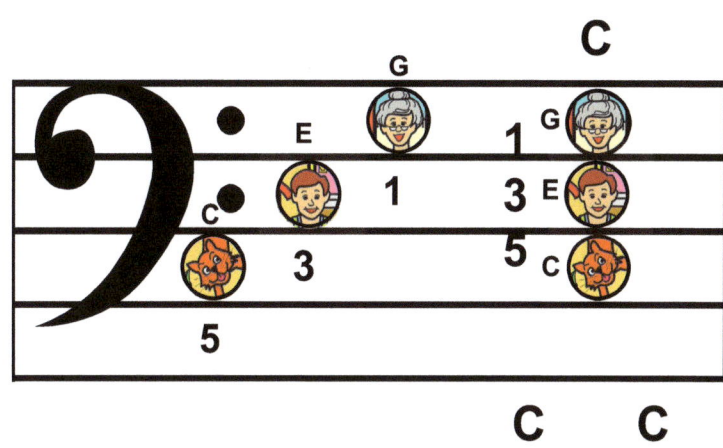
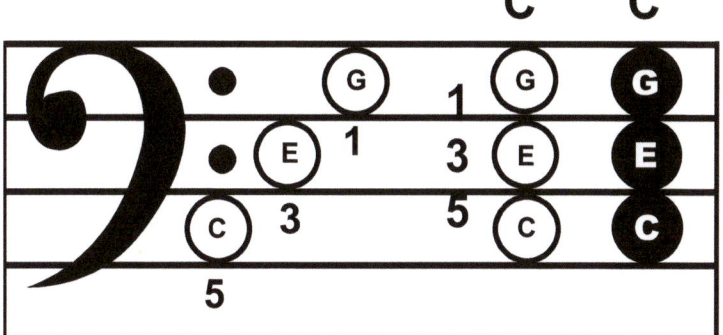
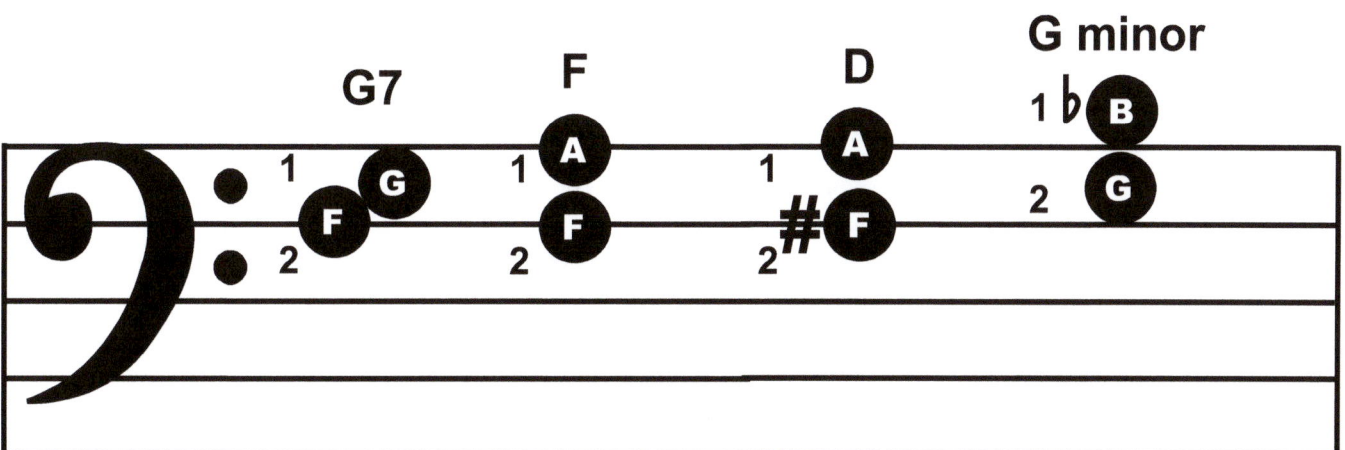
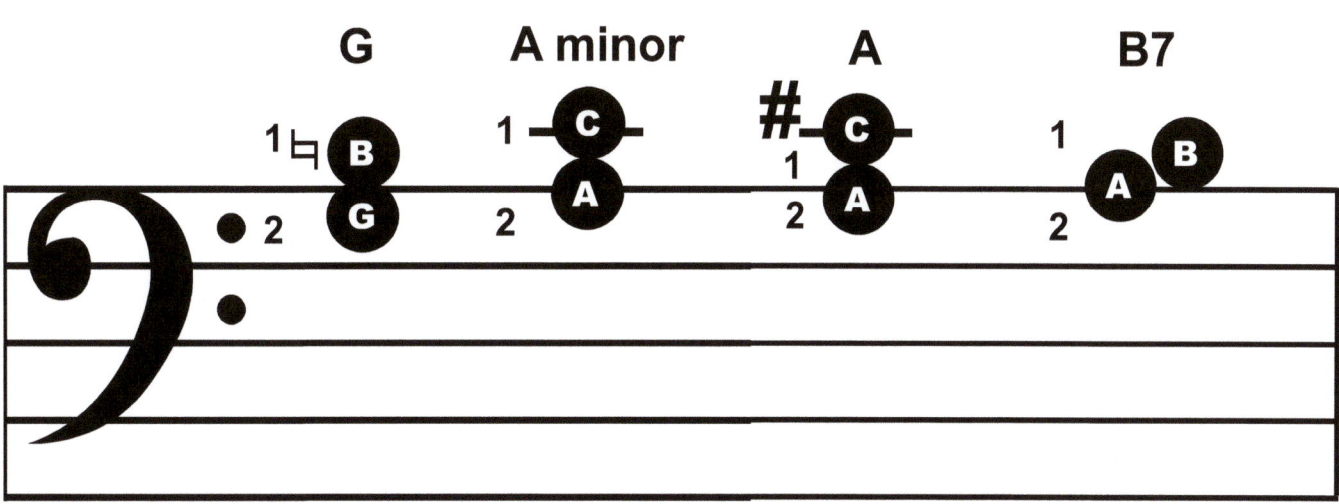

Counting Review

Counting is very important when you play piano.

Quarter notes get 1 count.
Or 1 piece of pizza when you cut the pizza into 4 slices.

Half notes get 2 counts.
Or 2 pieces of pizza.

Whole notes get 4 counts.
Or all 4 pieces of pizza. Notice that whole notes have no stems.

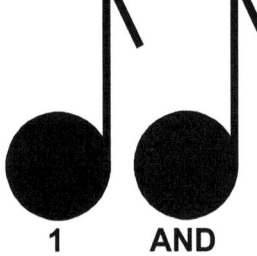

Eighth notes get 1/2 count.
You have to say "**1 AND**" when you count.

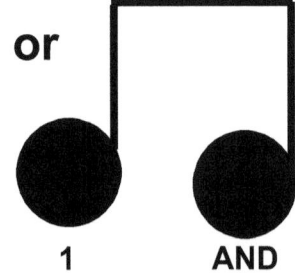

If several eighth notes are next to each other they are hooked together with a bridge.

Dots

Or chocolate drops. Take extra time to enjoy them.

When a "DOT" (or drop of chocolate as I call it) is placed after a note, give it extra time. Give it its count and another half of its count also.

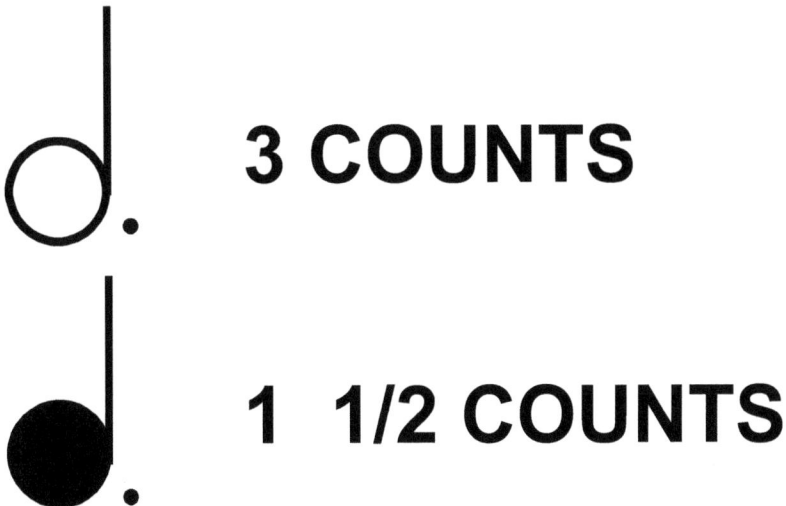

French Numbers
Les Nombres

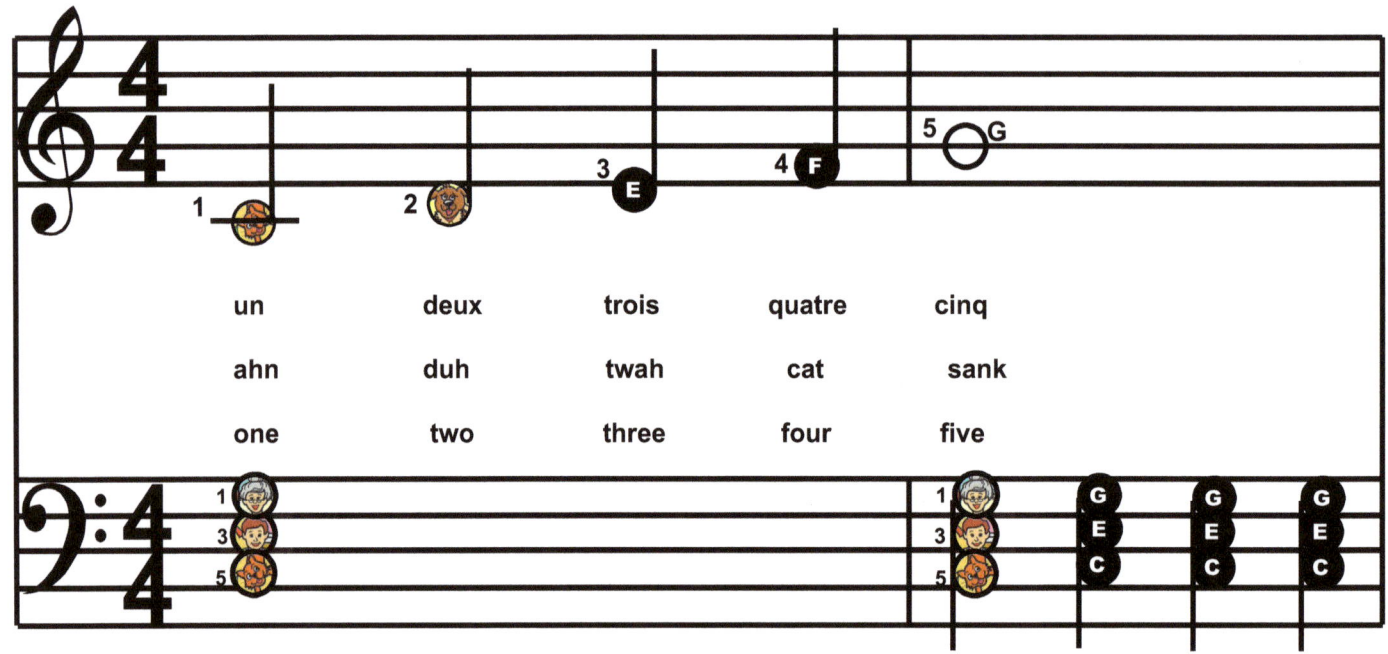

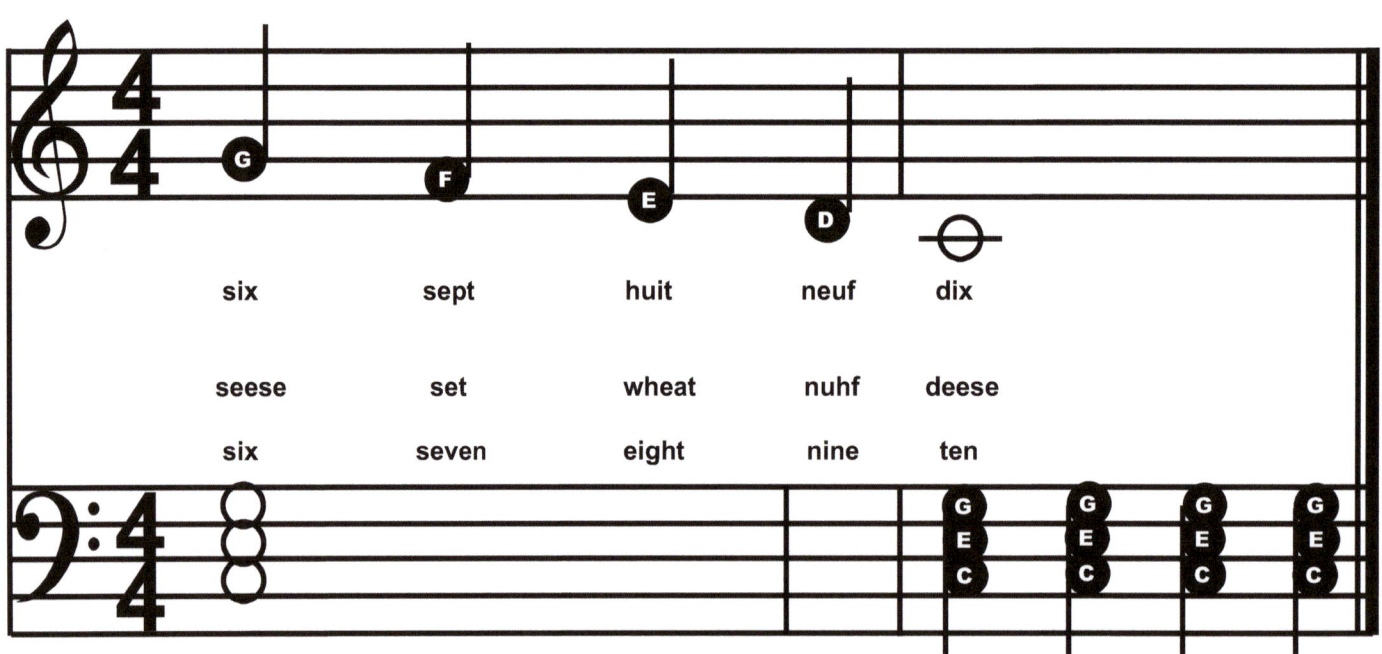

French Days of the Week
Jours de la semaine

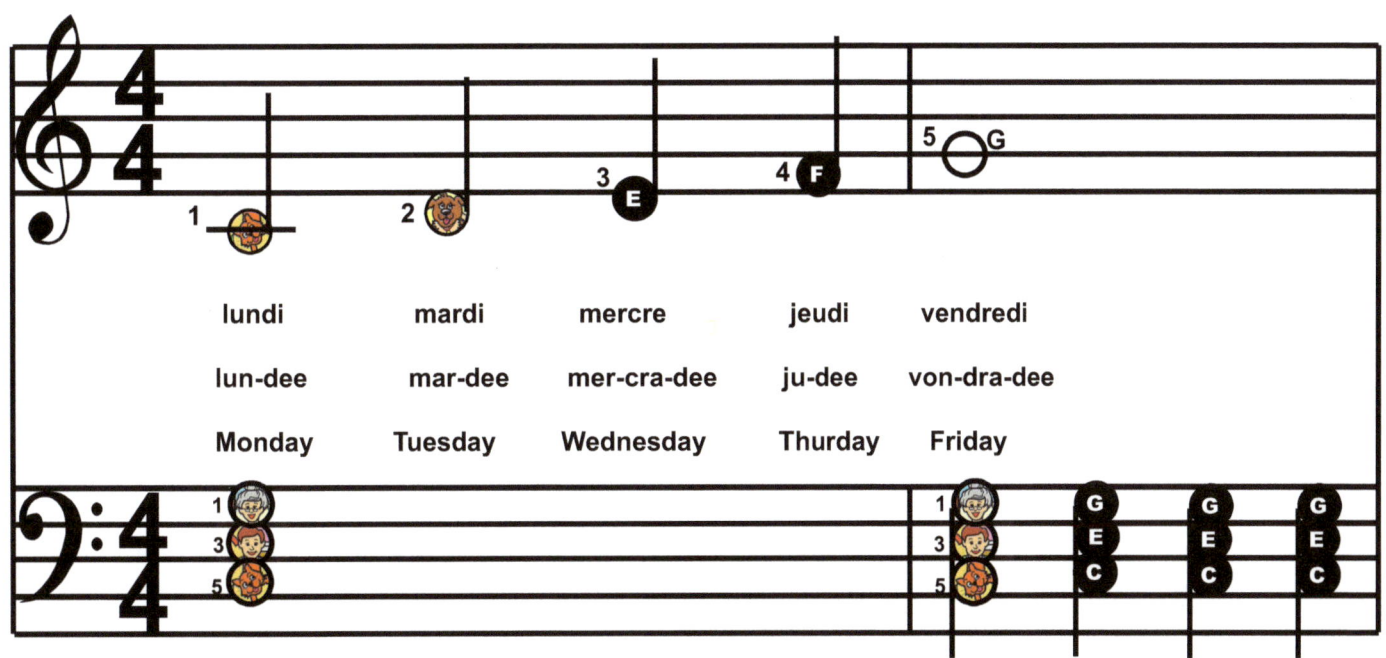

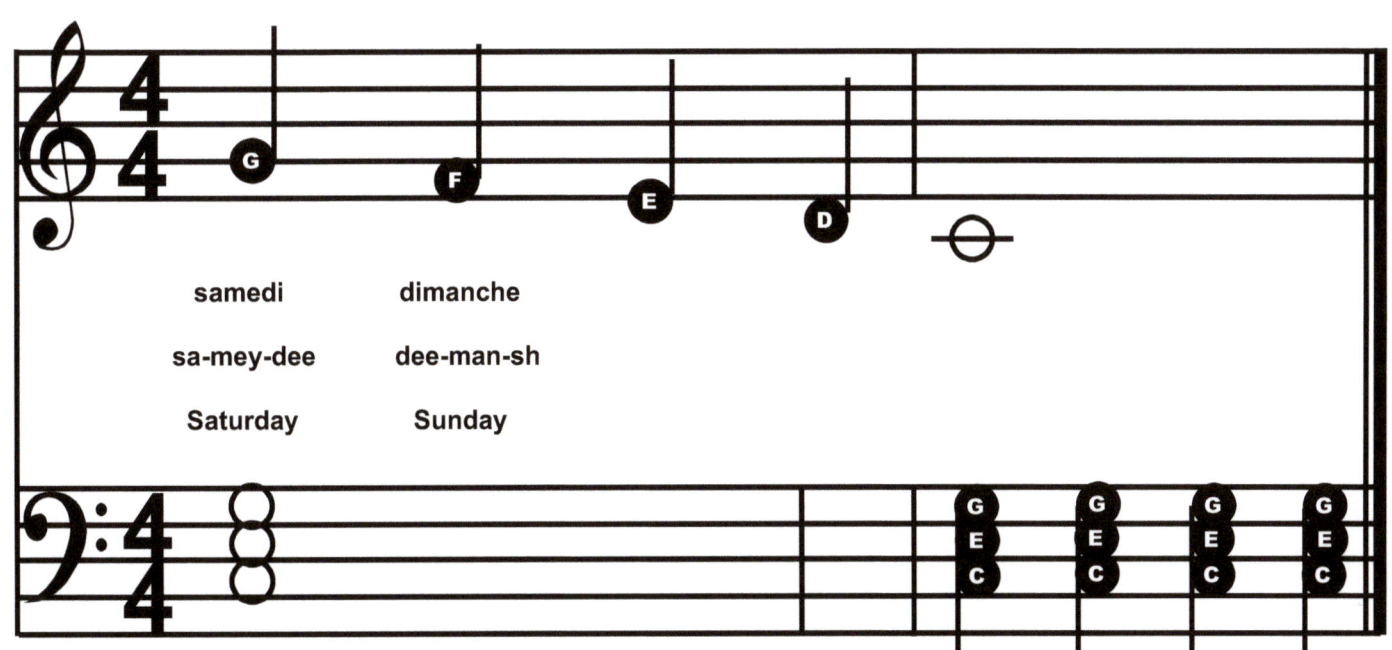

Traditional French

Frere Jacques
Brother John

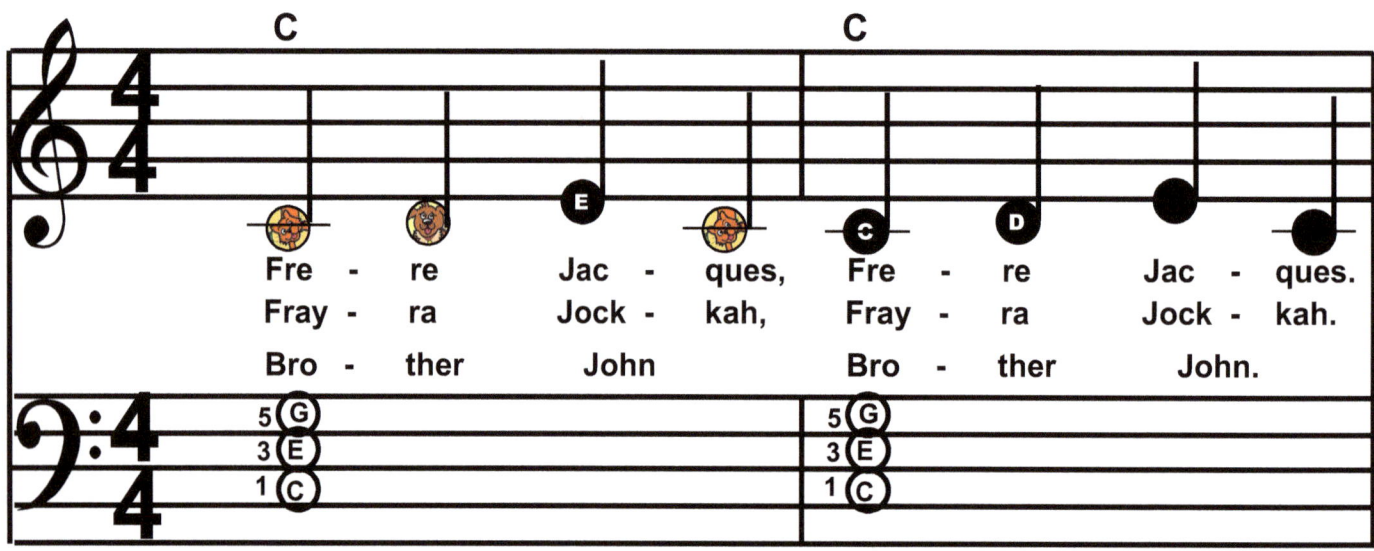

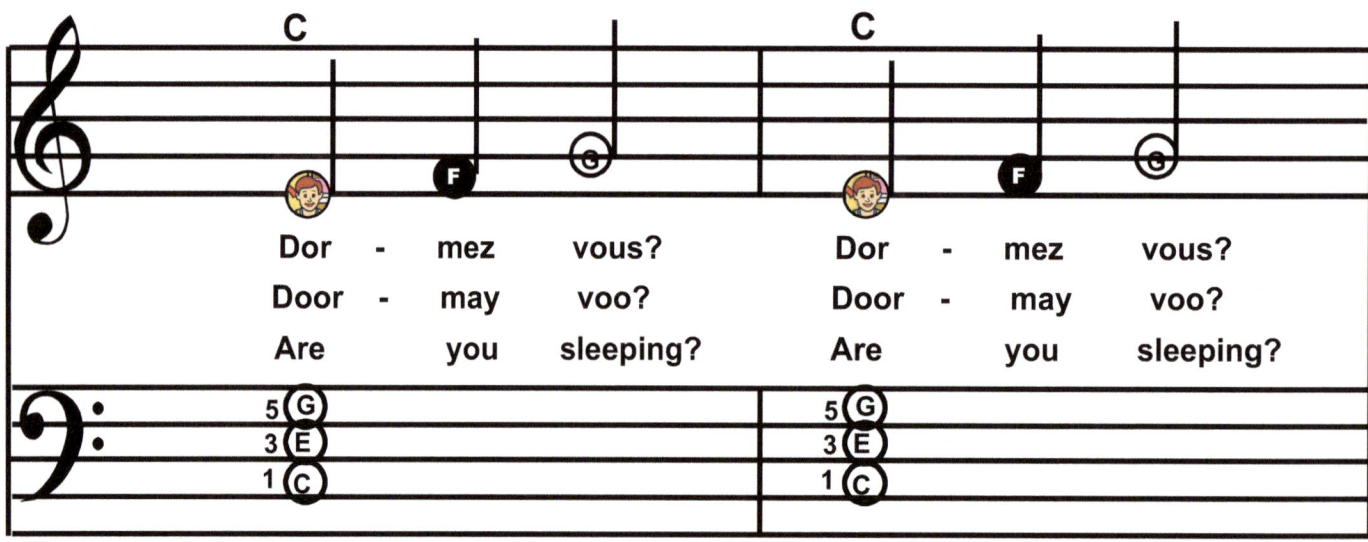

You will notice that in English these two lines of lyrics are sung in the opposite of the French. Also the order of words in French and English is sometimes reversed as often happens in Spanish as well. Dormez vous literally is "sleeping you?"

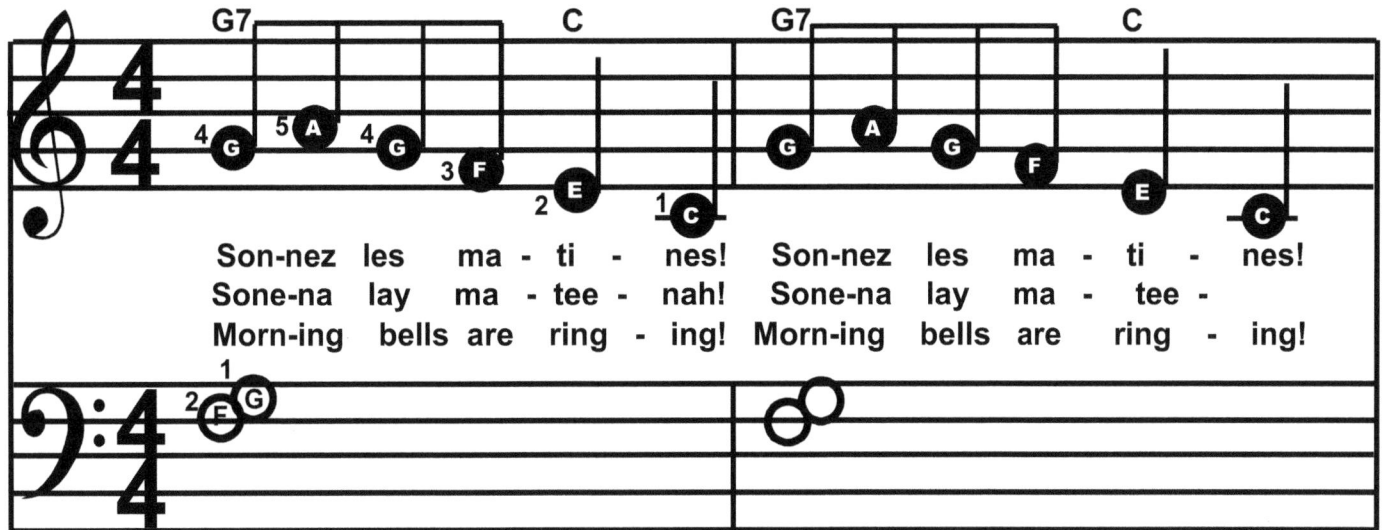

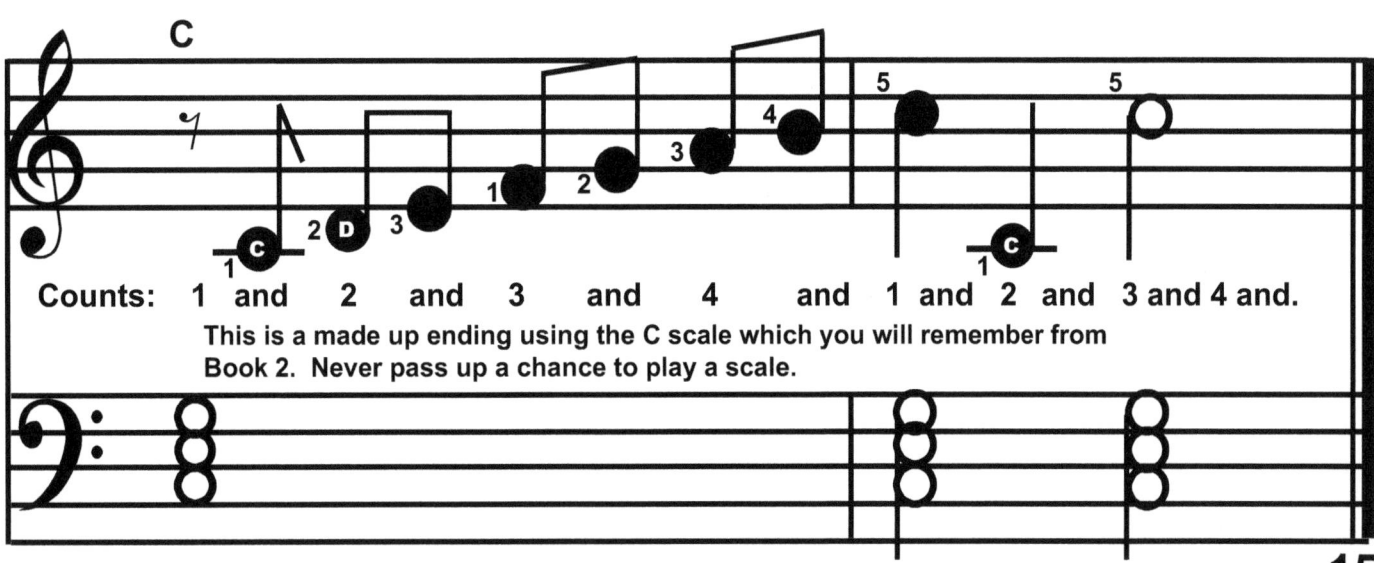

This is a made up ending using the C scale which you will remember from Book 2. Never pass up a chance to play a scale.

Alouette
The Lark

French Folk Song

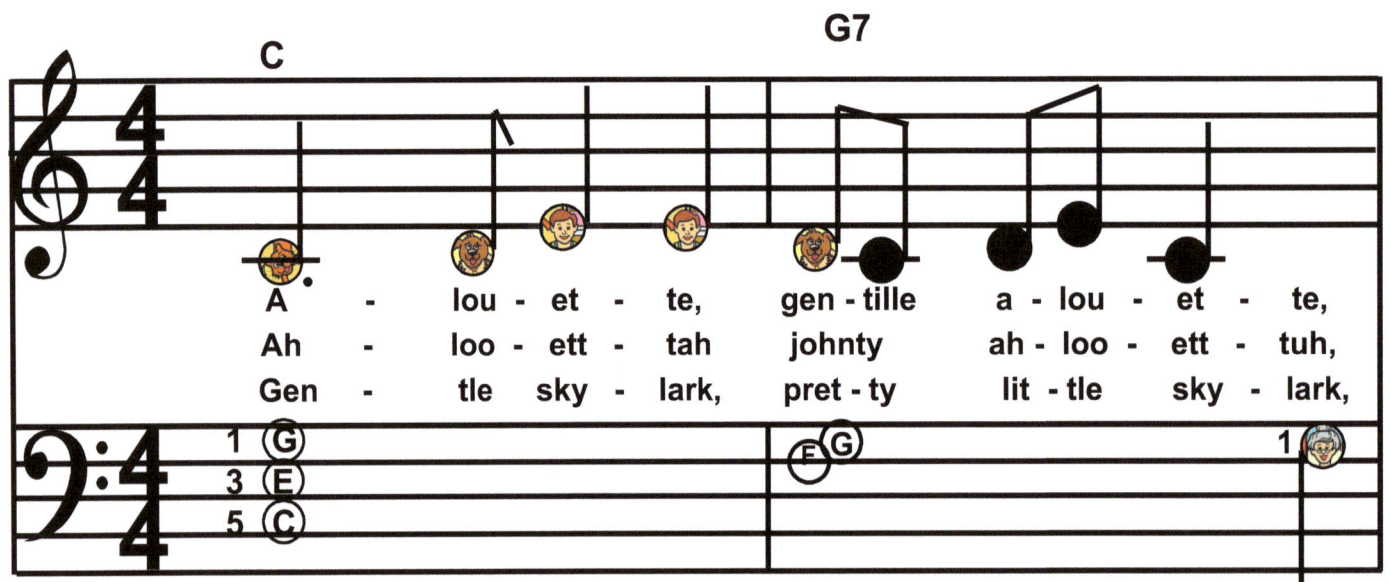

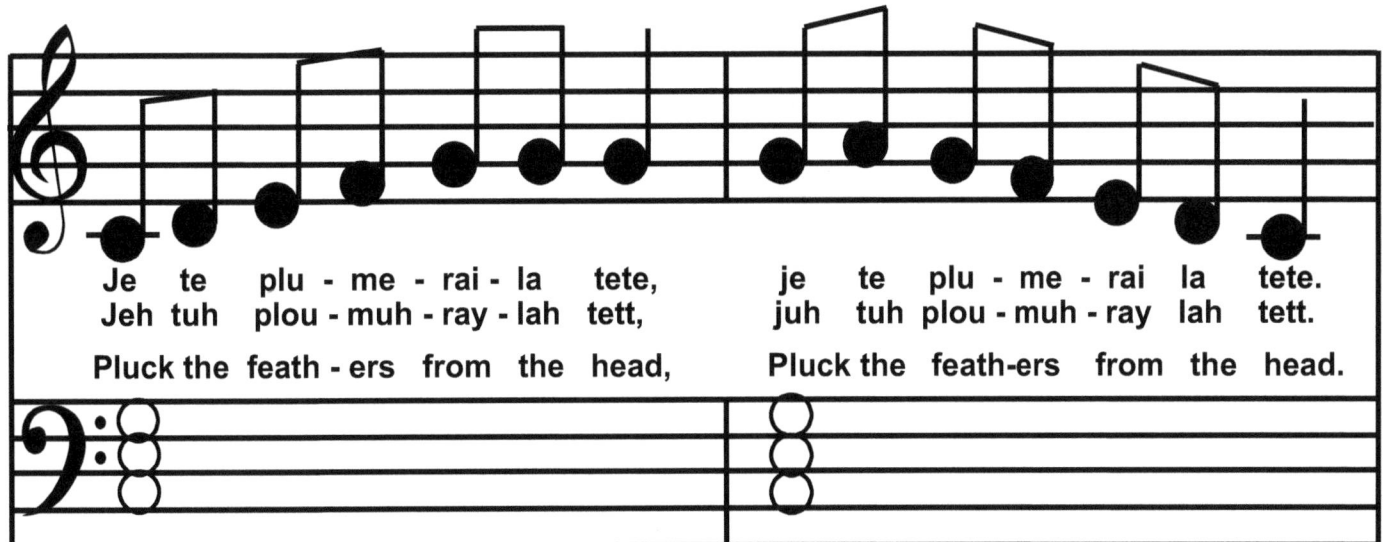

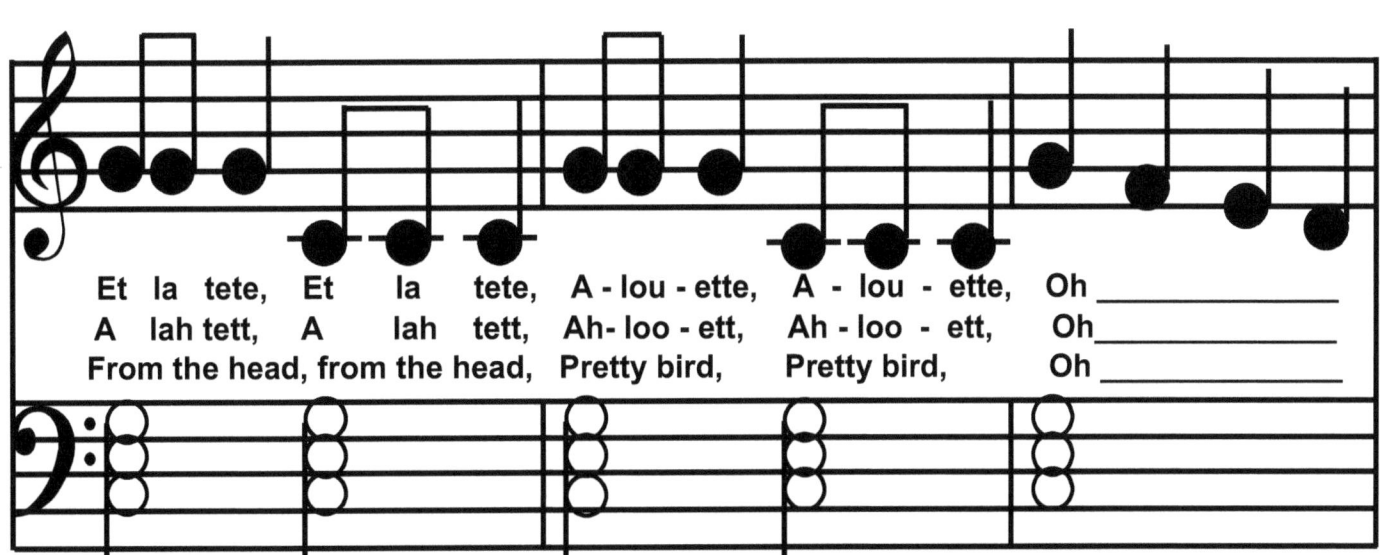

Repeat the first page then sing the next verse replacing the word "head" in the lyrics with the word for the 2nd verse, and so on.

2. **Le bec**
   Luh beck
   The beck

3. **Le cou**
   Luh coo
   The neck

4. **Le dos**
   Luh doh
   The back

5. **La jambe**
   Lah jumb
   The leg

6. **Le pied**
   Luh pee ay
   The foot

7. **Make up your own**

La Cucaracha
The Cockroach

Watch for the B Flat and the fingering. Use the C chord and the F chord short version that you learned in Picture Songs Book 2.

Spanish Folk Song

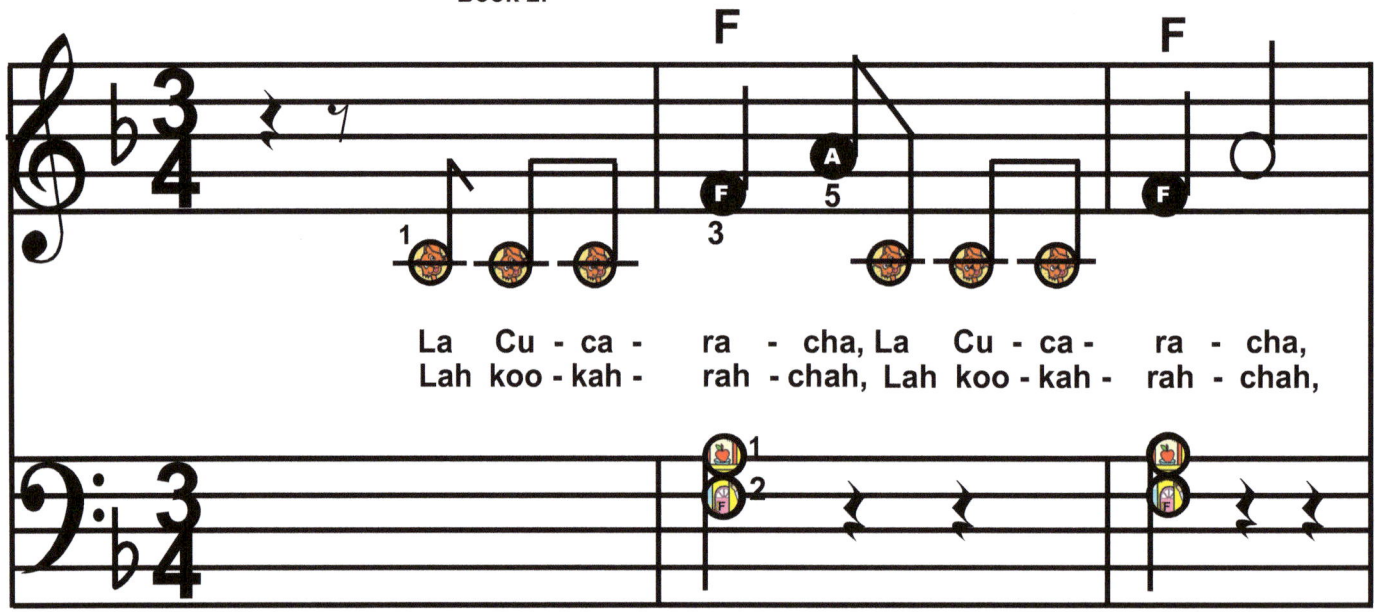

La Cu - ca - ra - cha, La Cu - ca - ra - cha,
Lah koo - kah - rah - chah, Lah koo - kah - rah - chah,

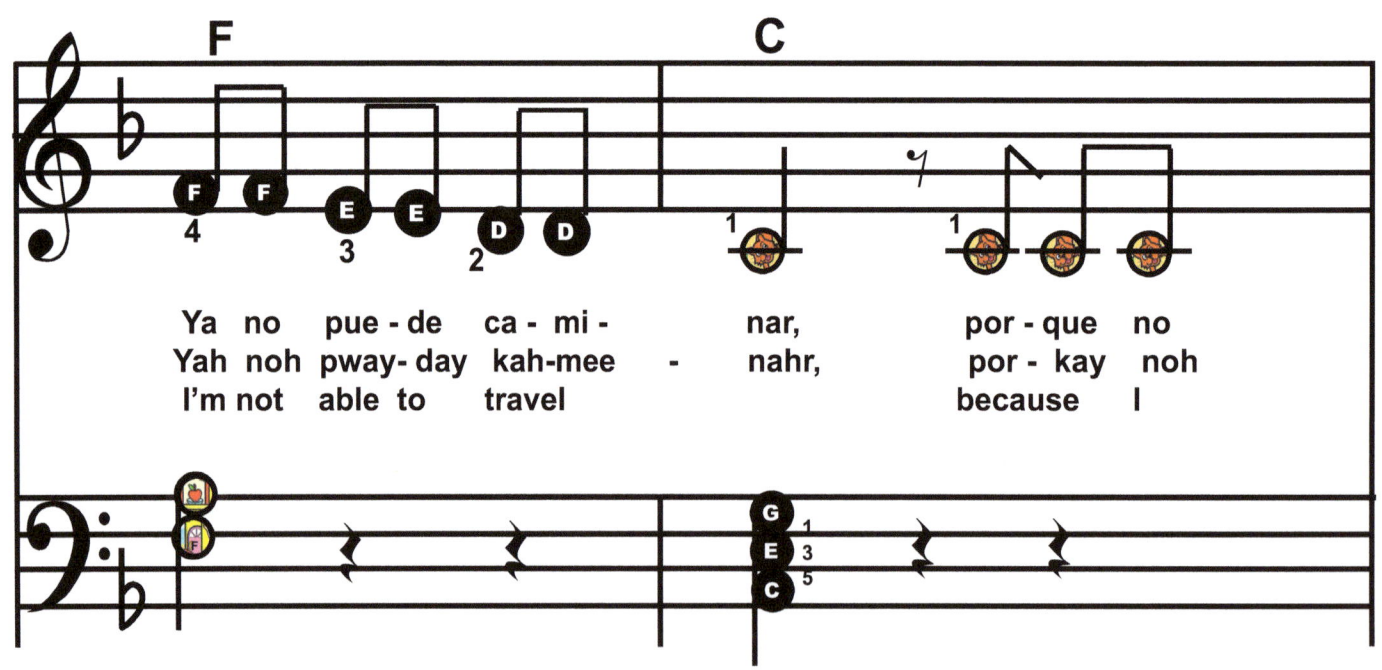

Ya no pue - de ca - mi - nar, por - que no
Yah noh pway - day kah - mee - nahr, por - kay noh
I'm not able to travel because I

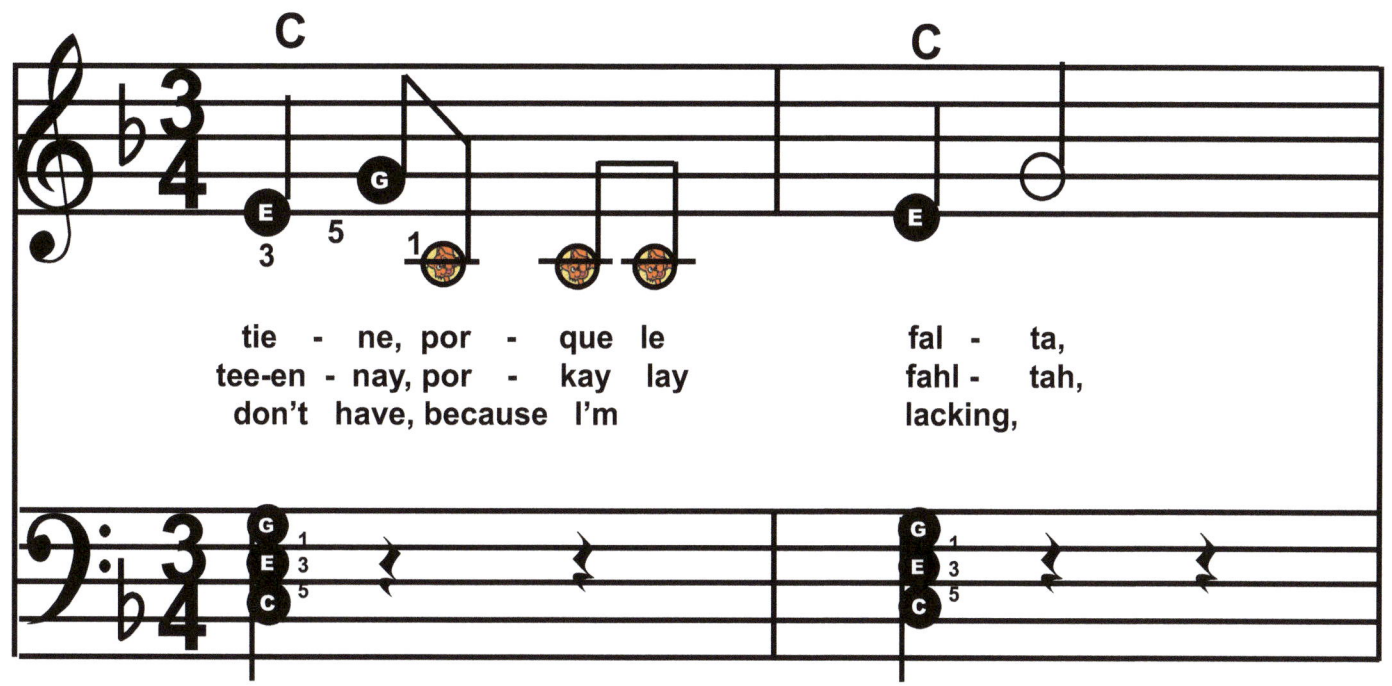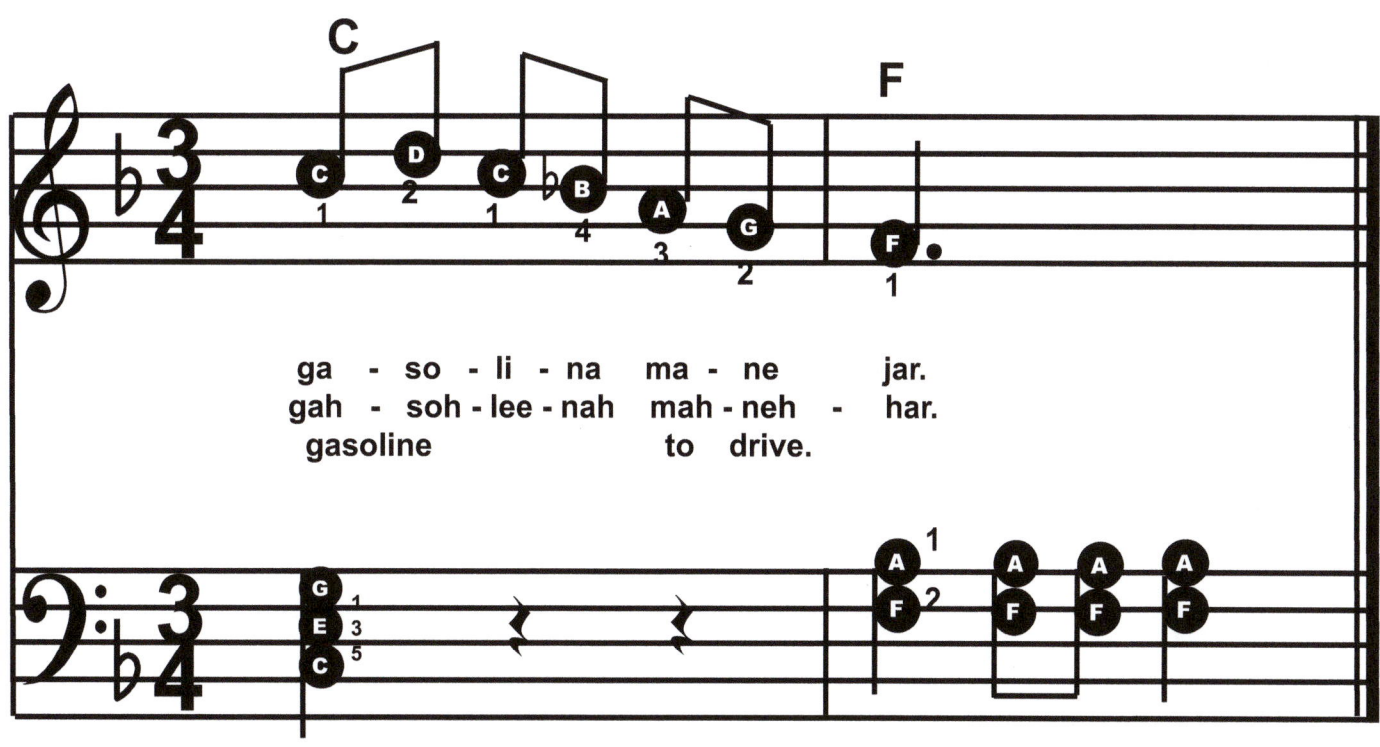

Las Mañanitas

Mexican Folk Song 1896
Composer unknown

Hand postition: Both first fingers (thumbs) share middle C. Watch out for the left hand notes especially the first 2 notes of the song.

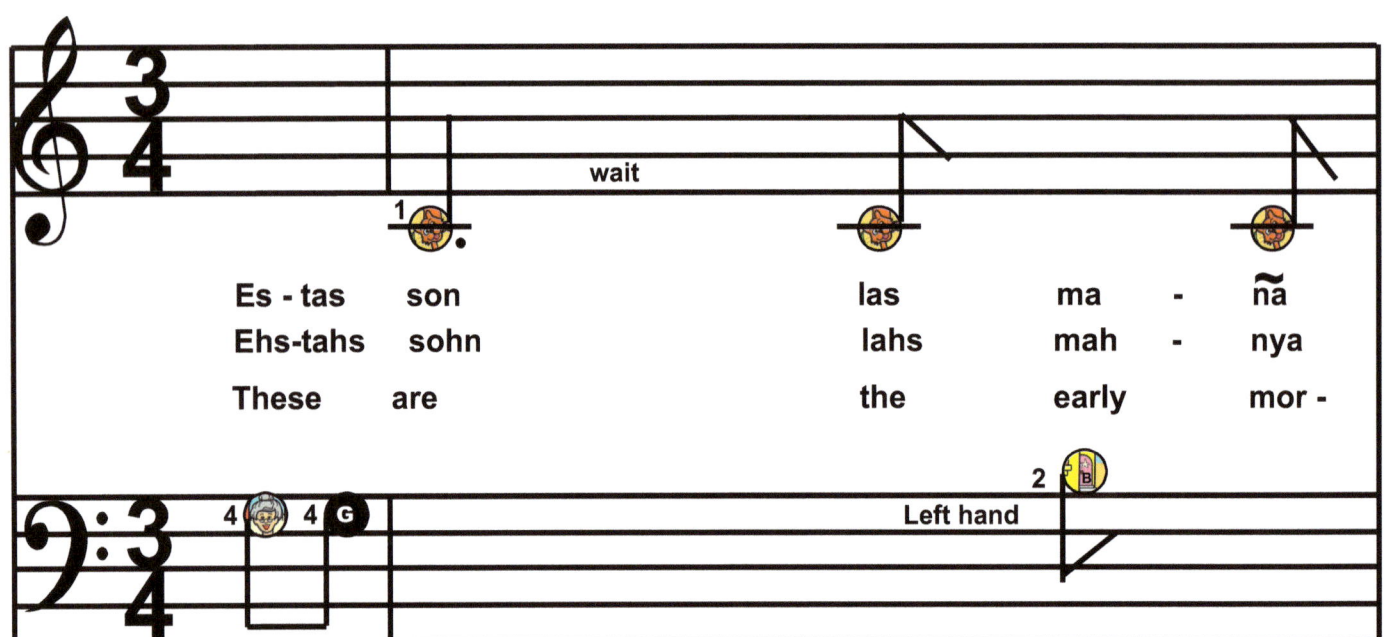

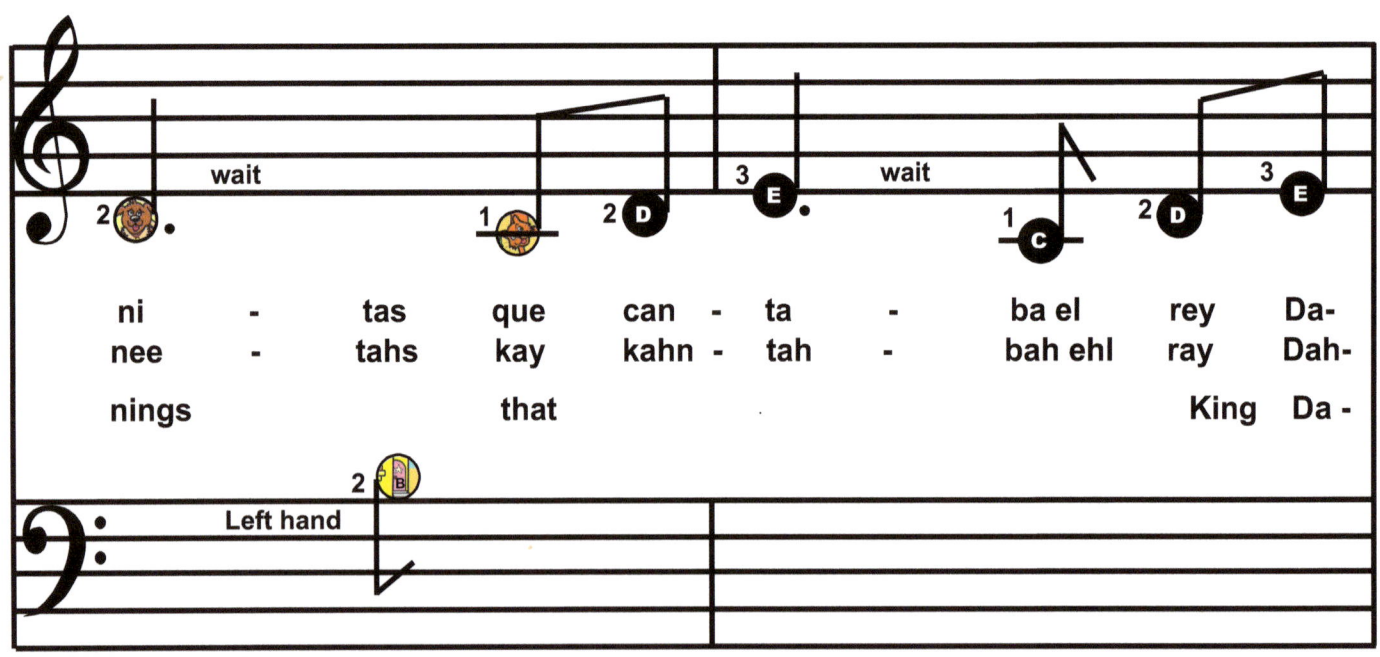

20

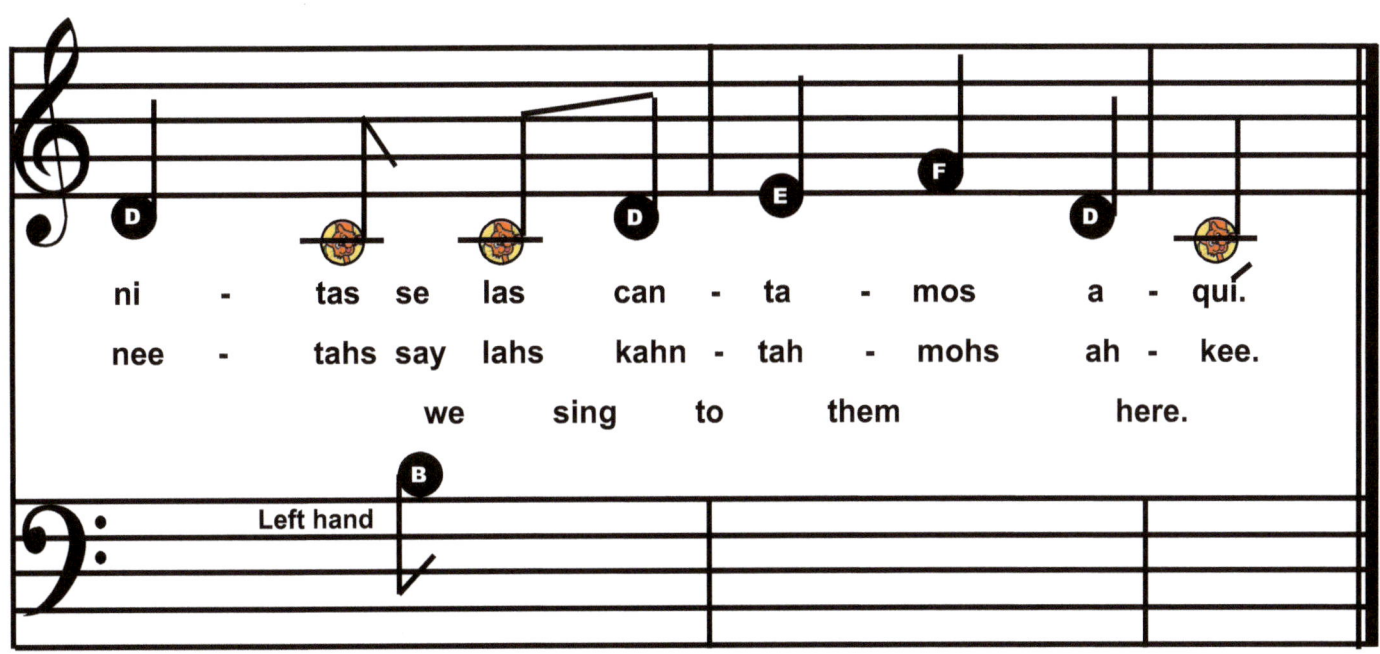

Troll Mom's Lullaby
Swedish

Lena Orbelius

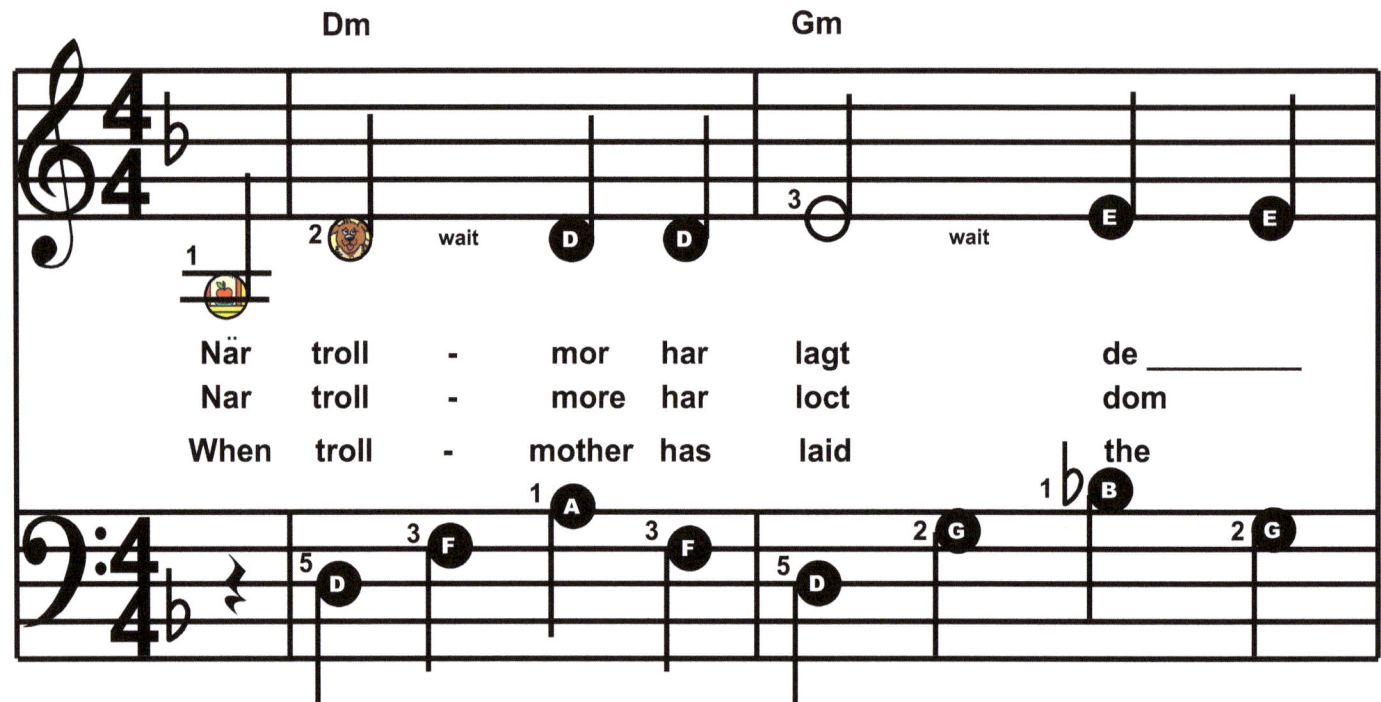

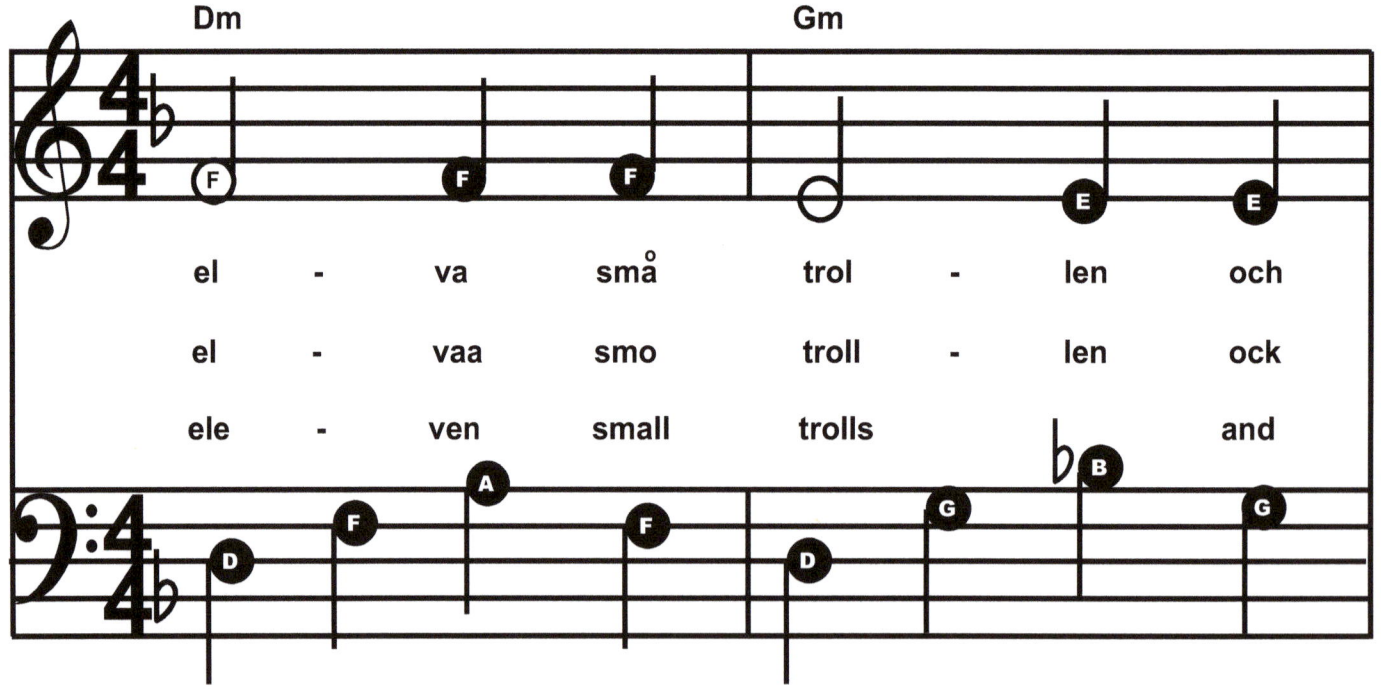

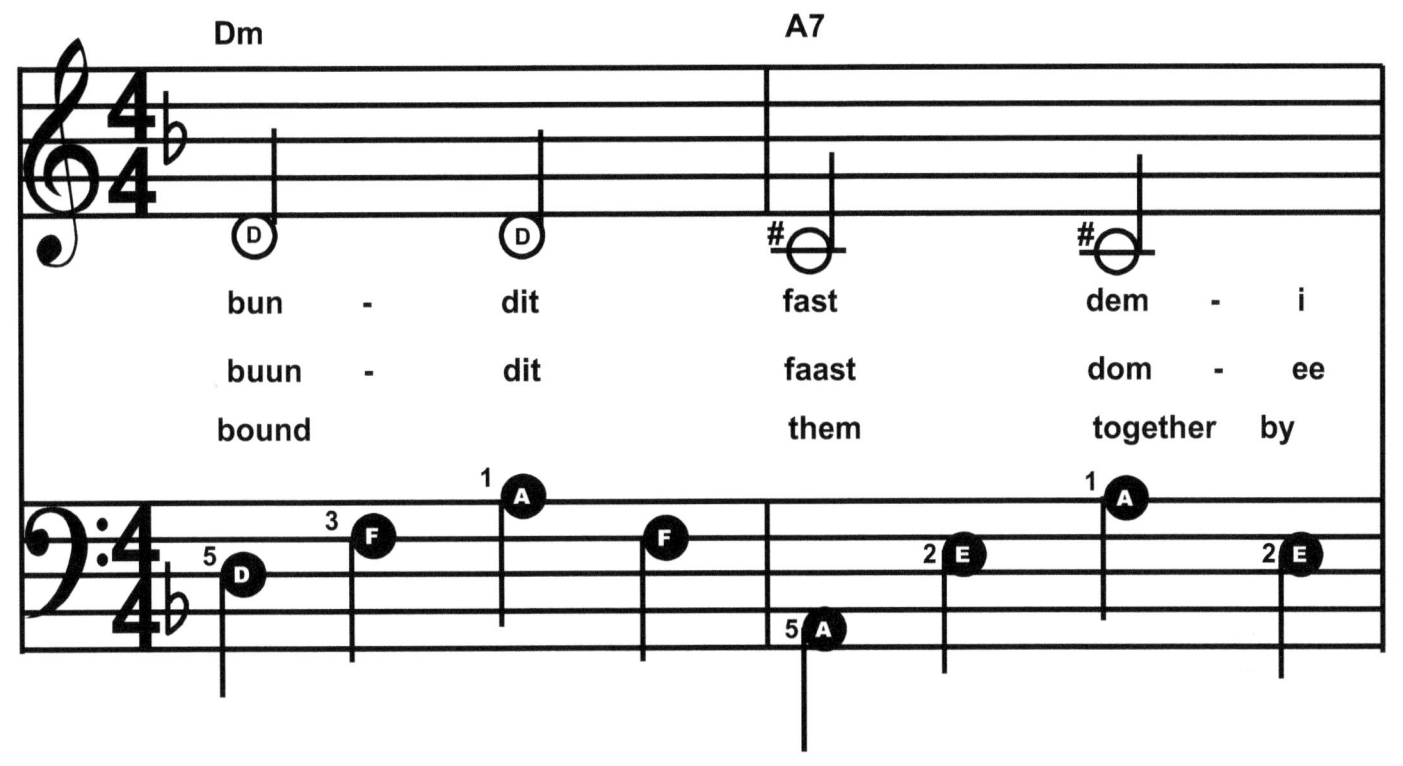
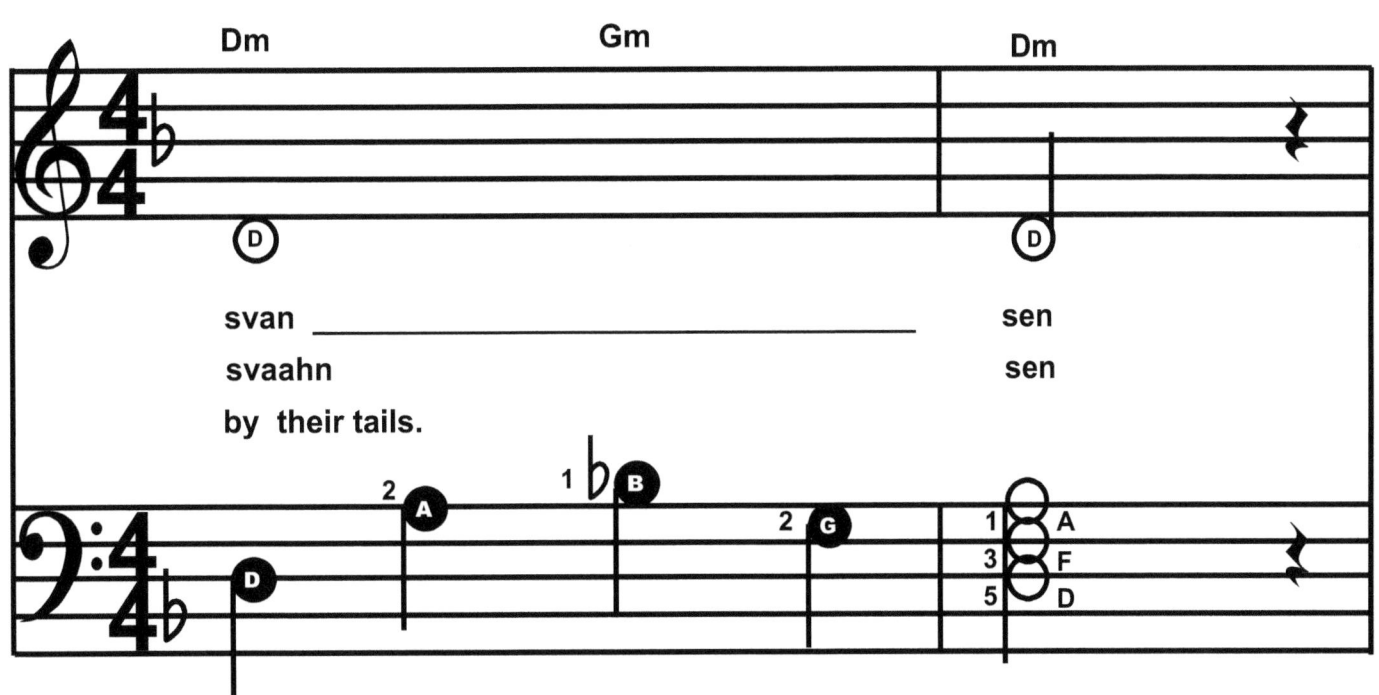

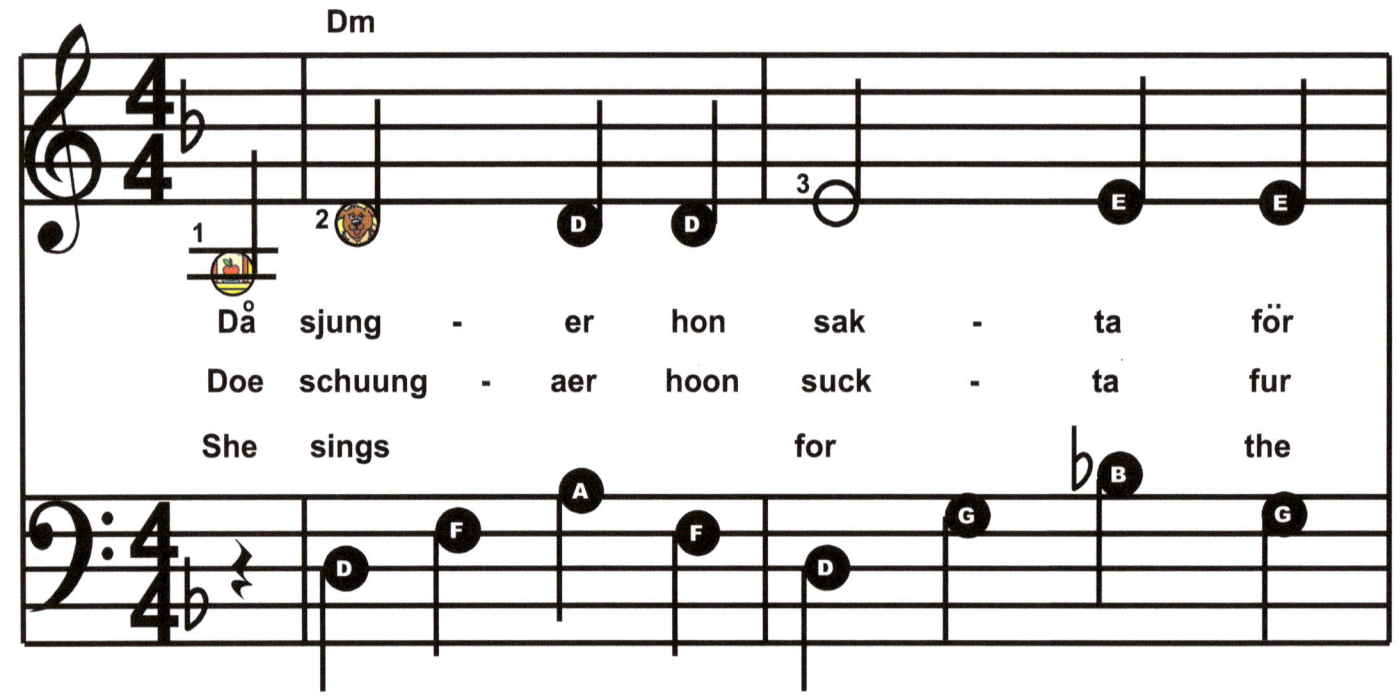
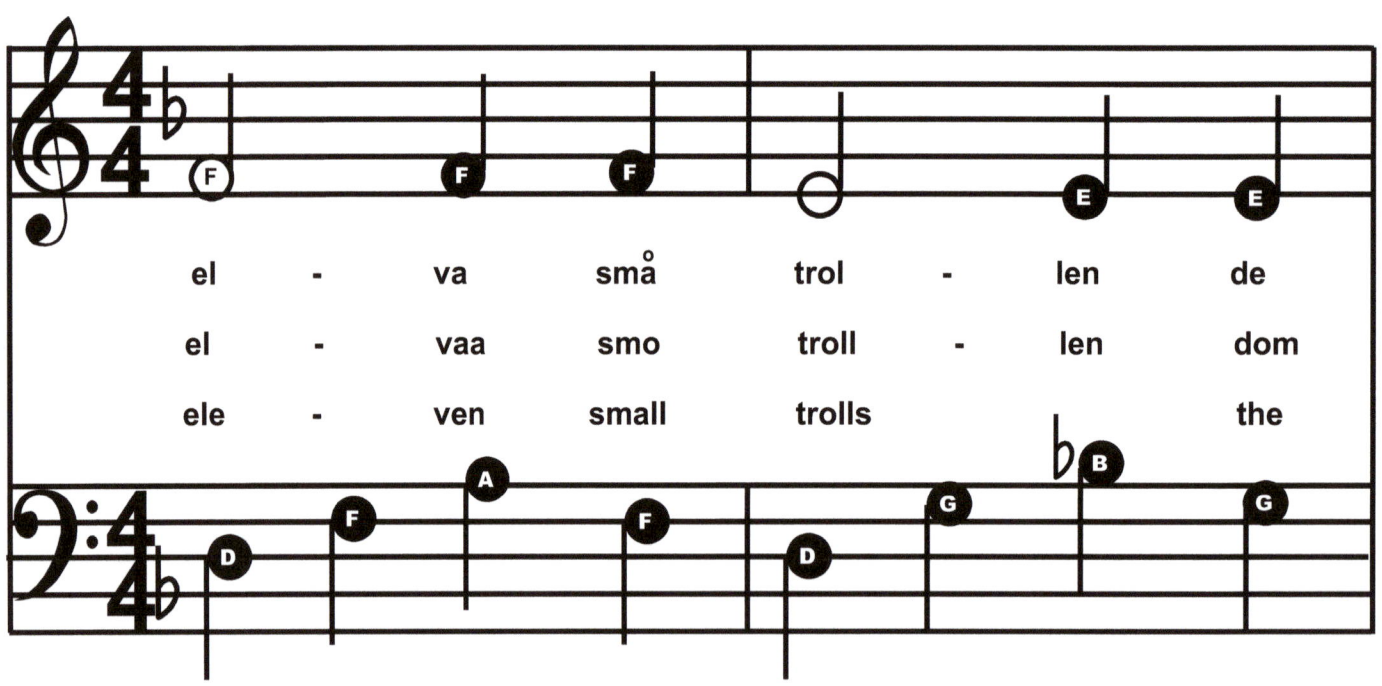

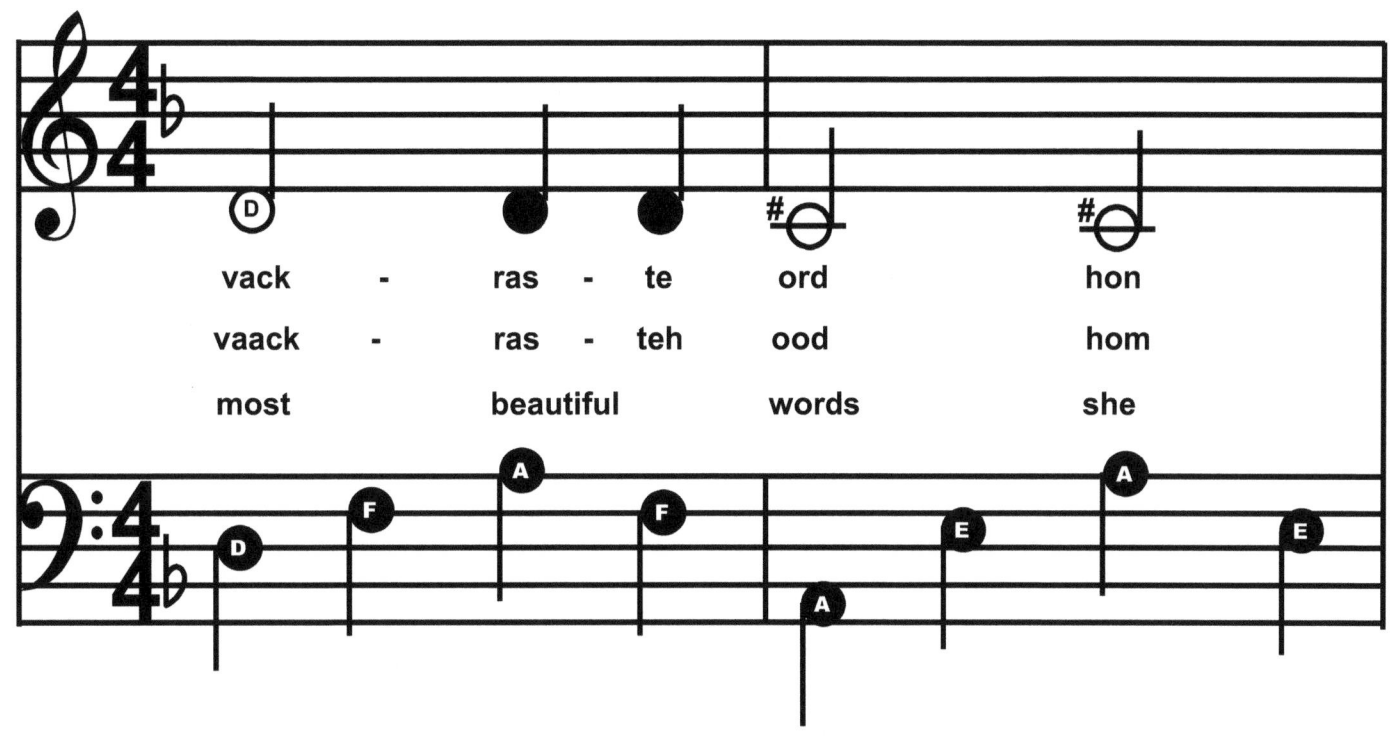
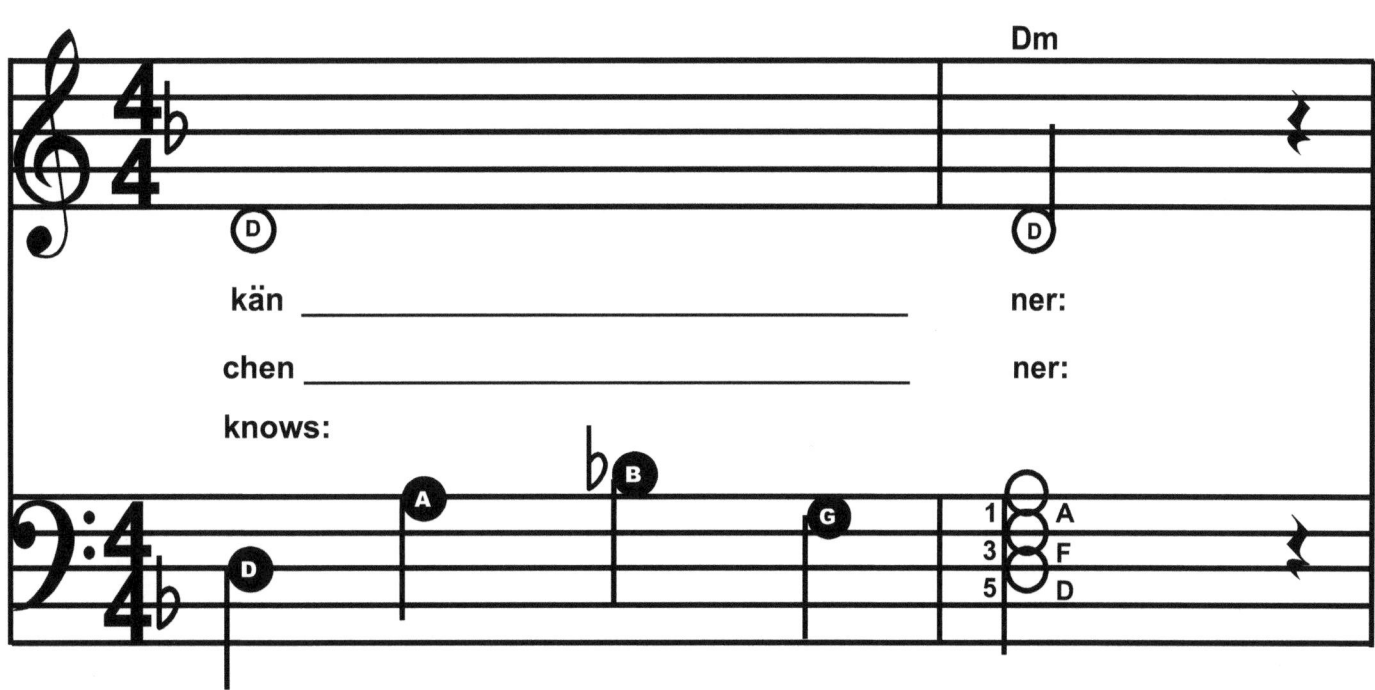

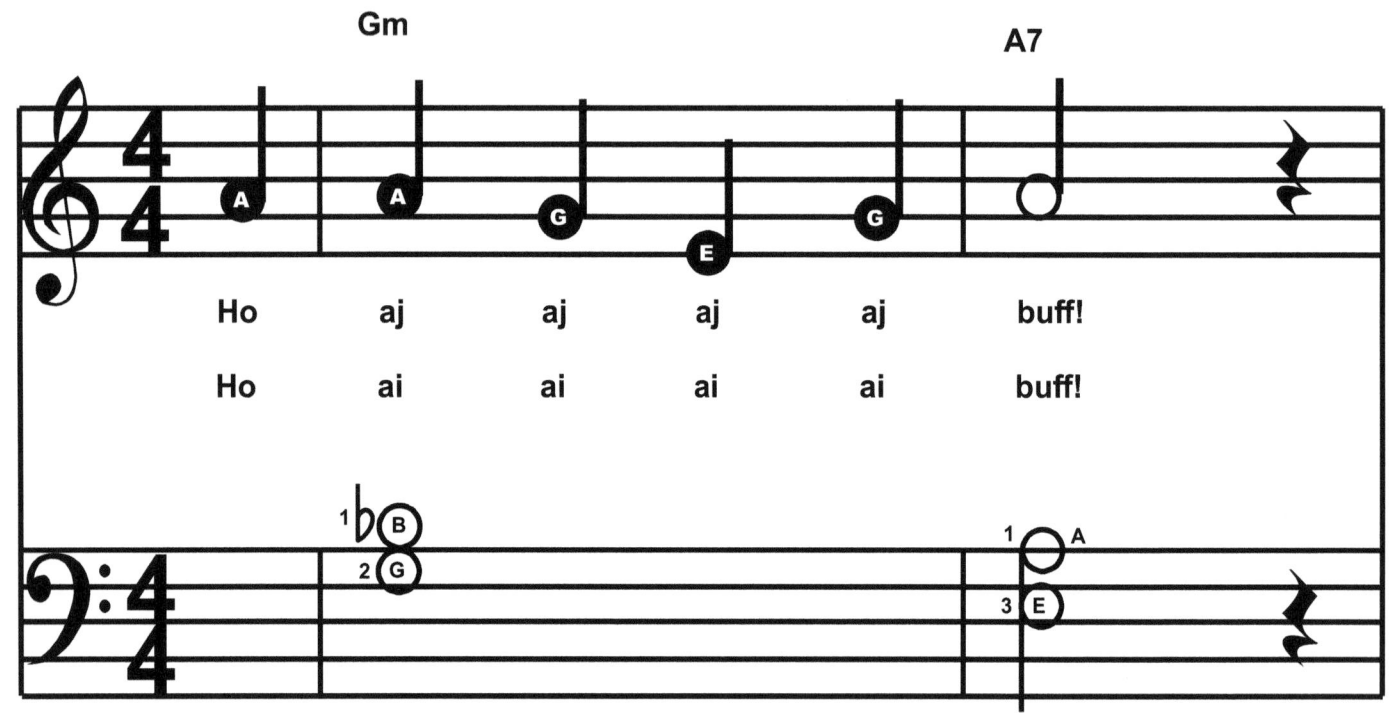
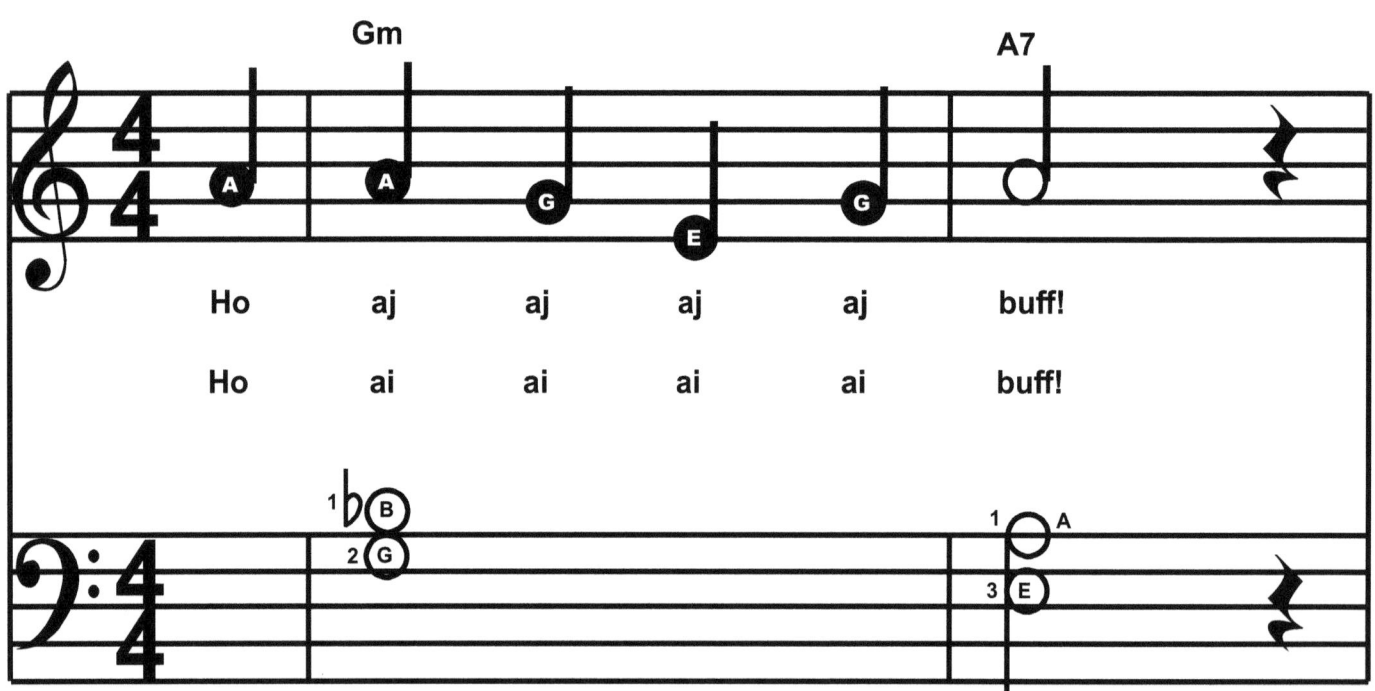

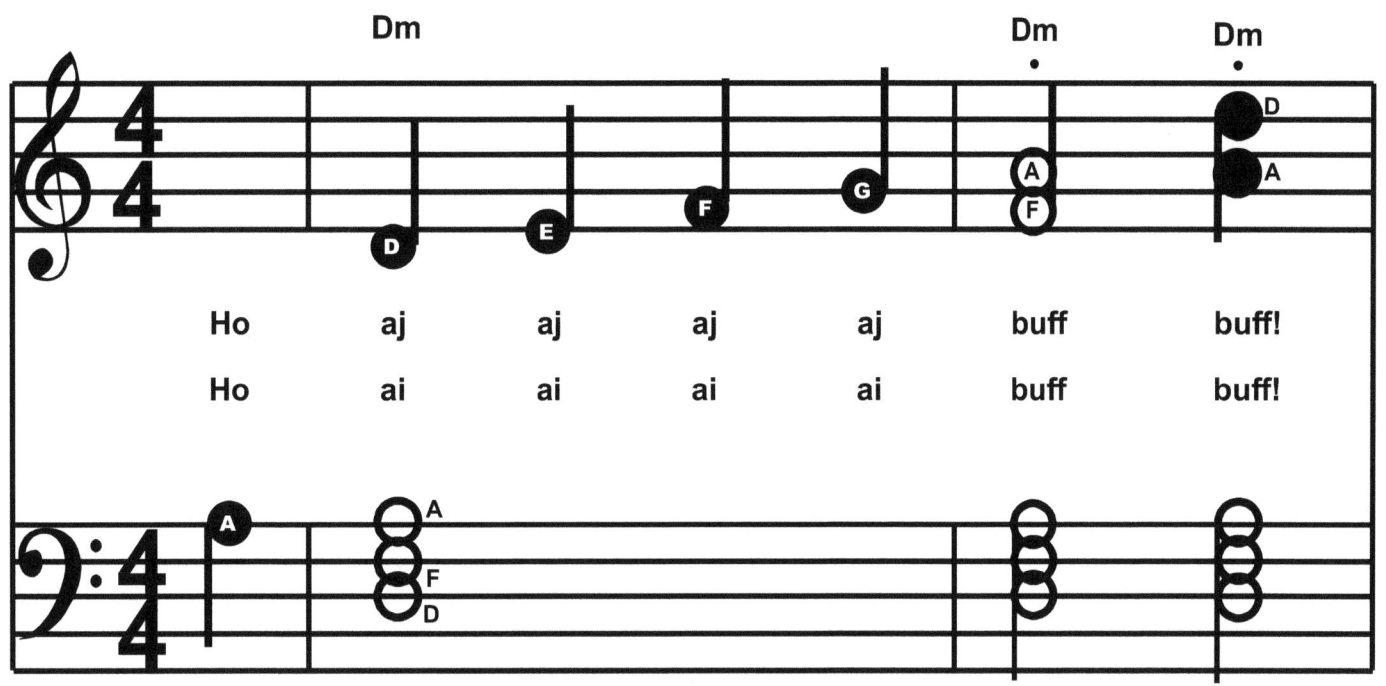

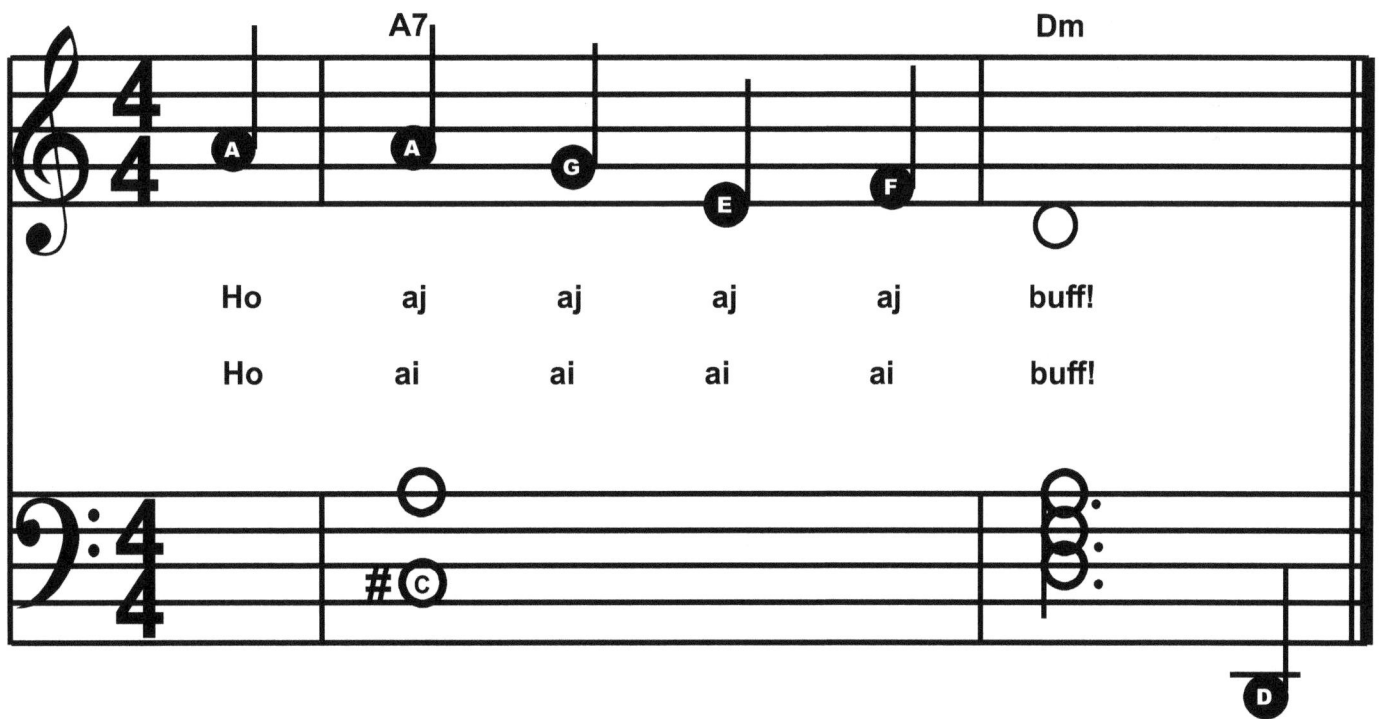

Wiegenlied
Cradle Song

Johannes Brahms

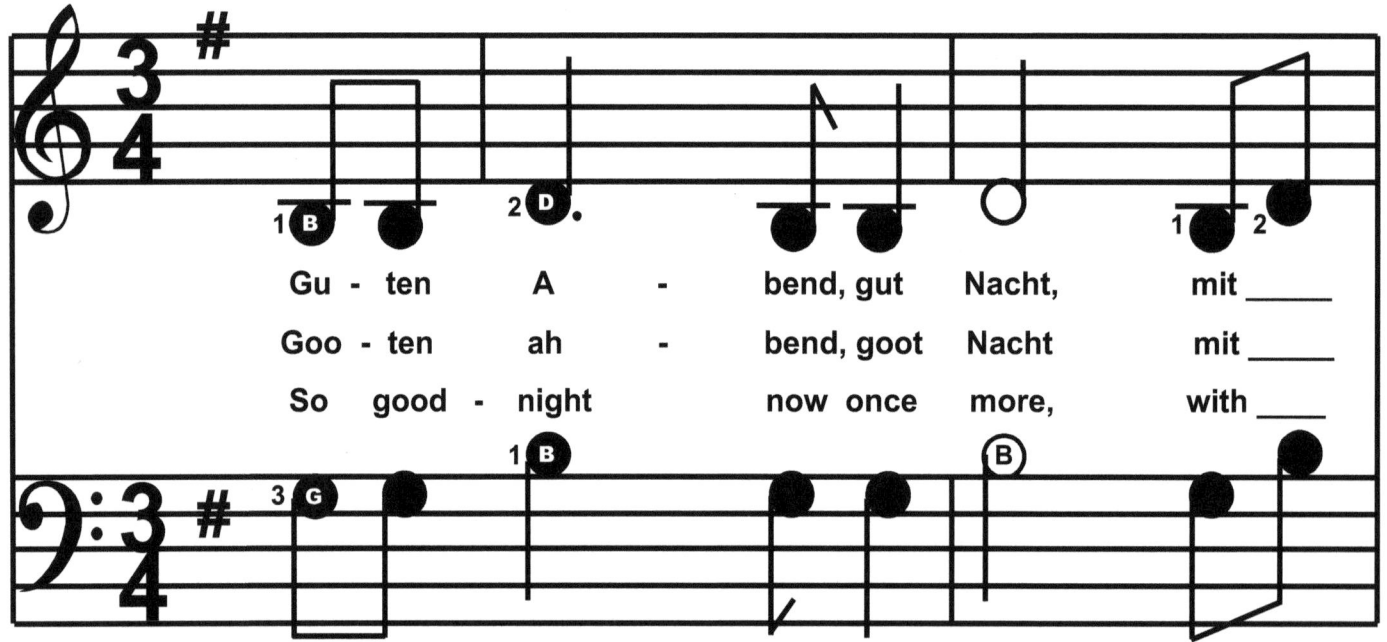

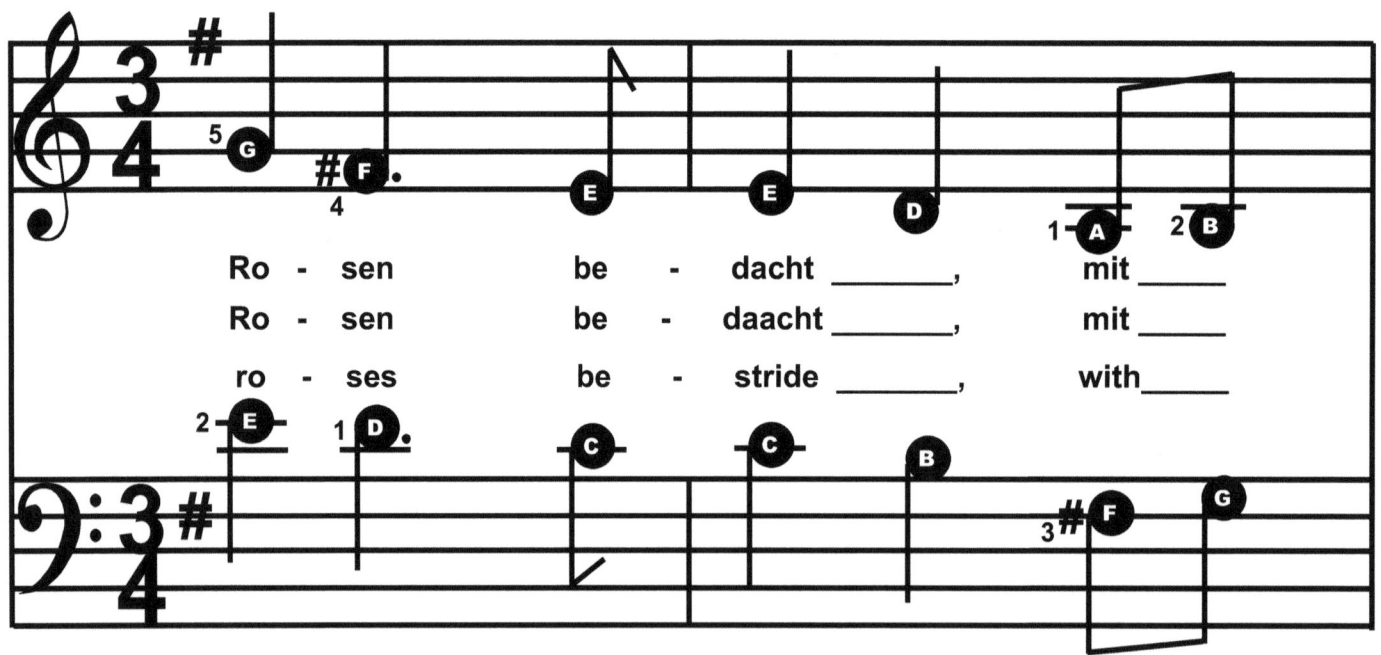

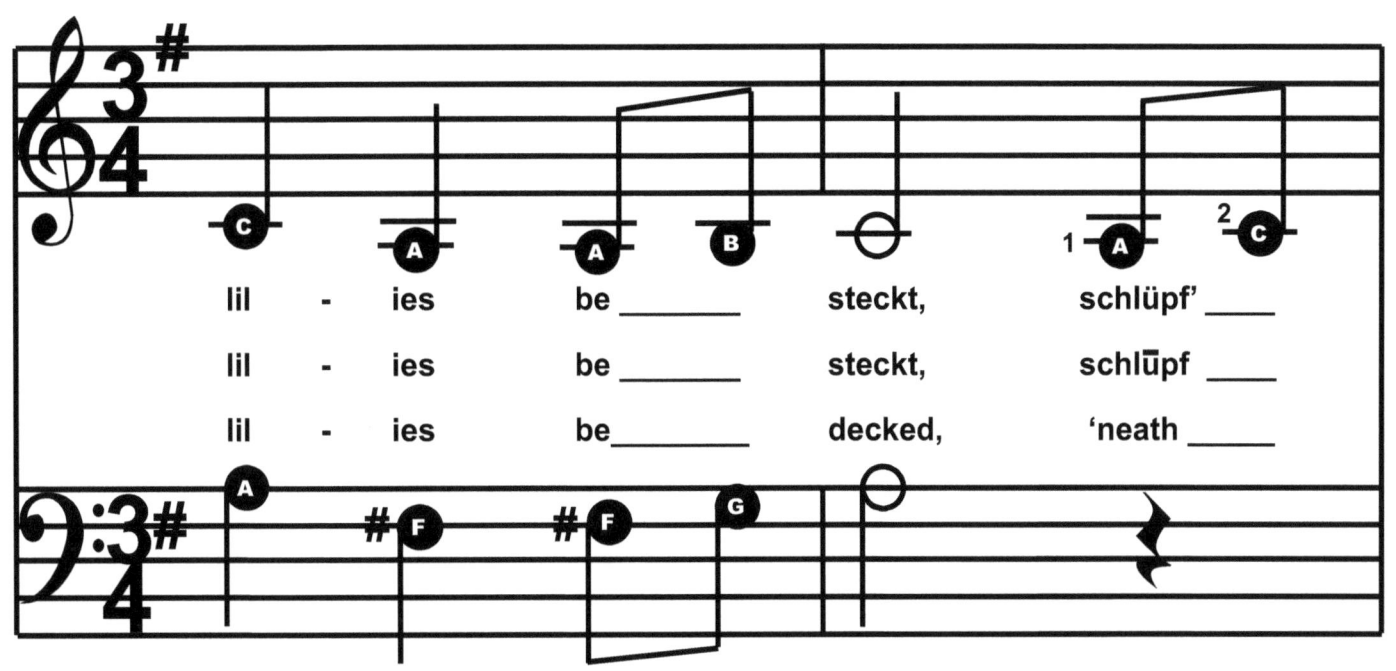
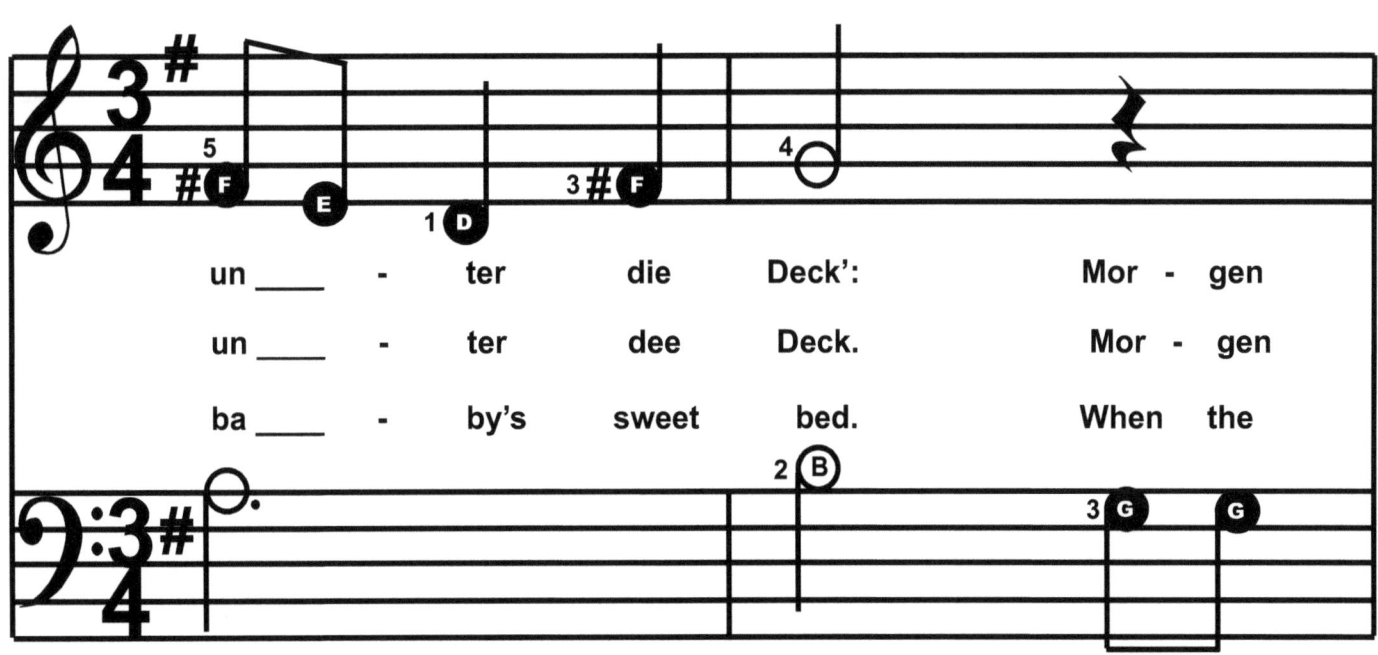

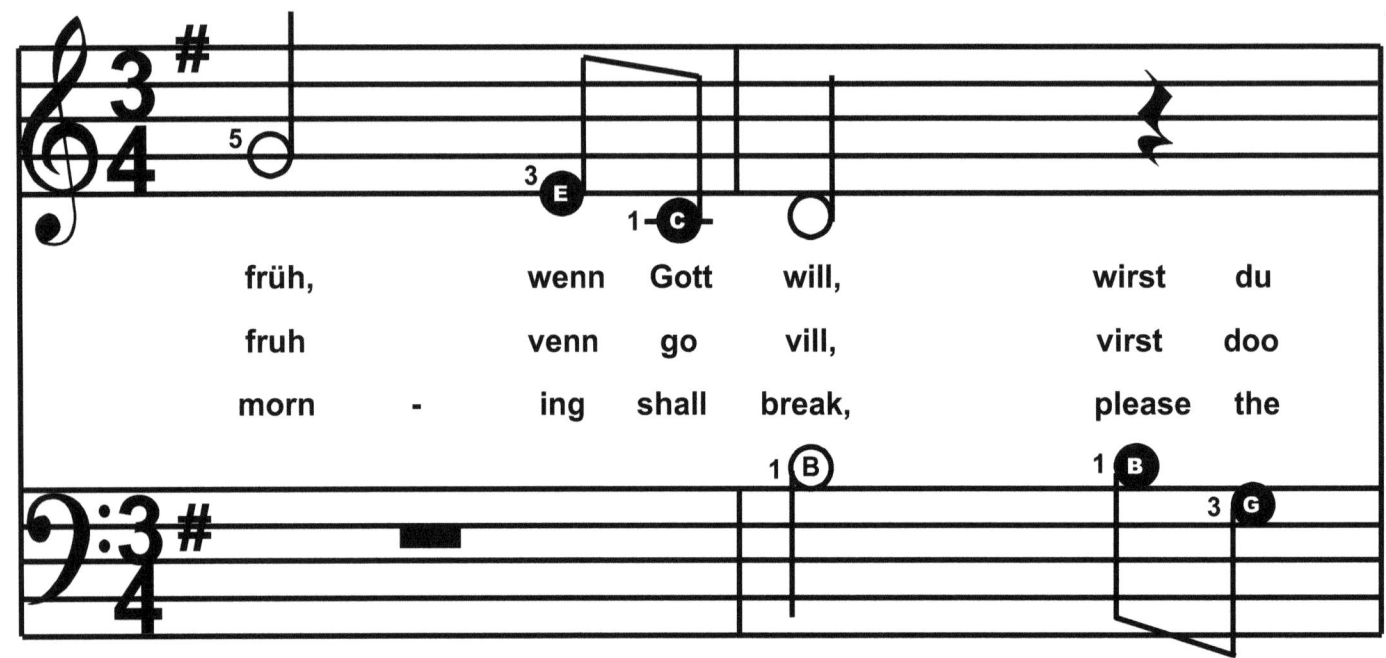

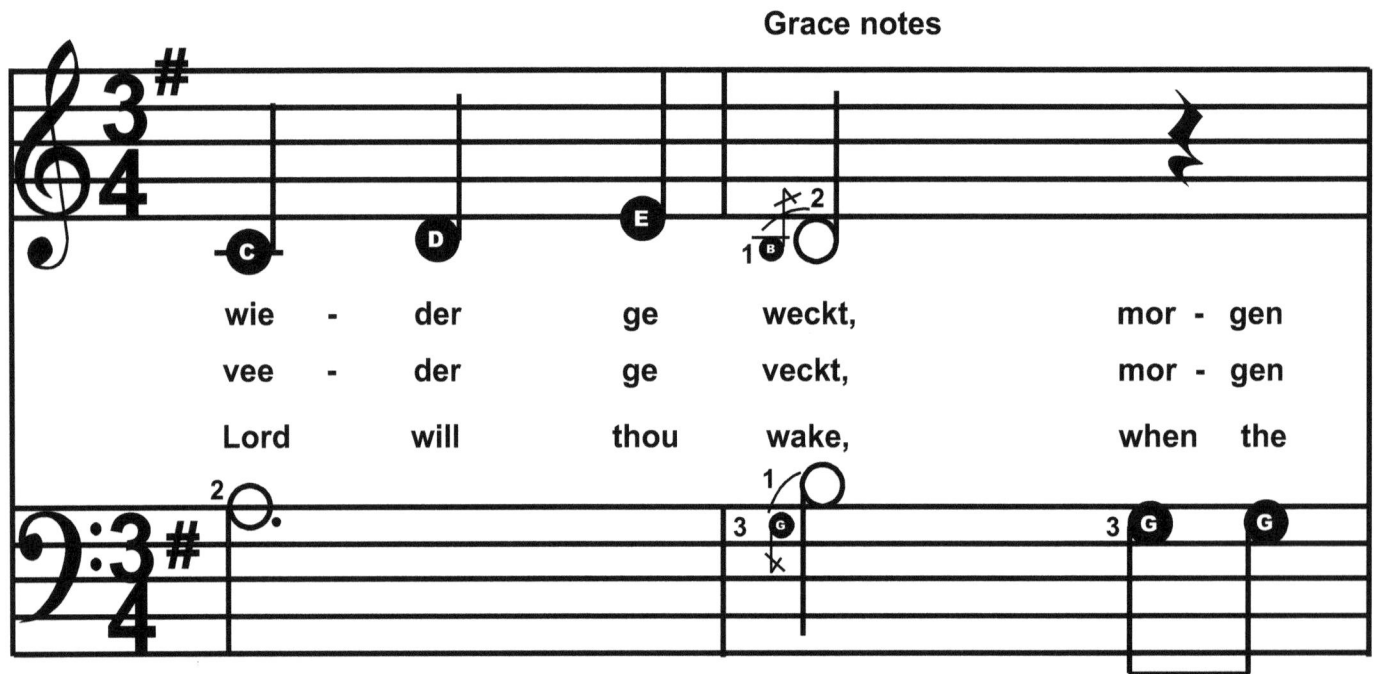

Grace notes - When you see tiny notes hooked to regular notes as above, play the little notes really fast before the regular note.

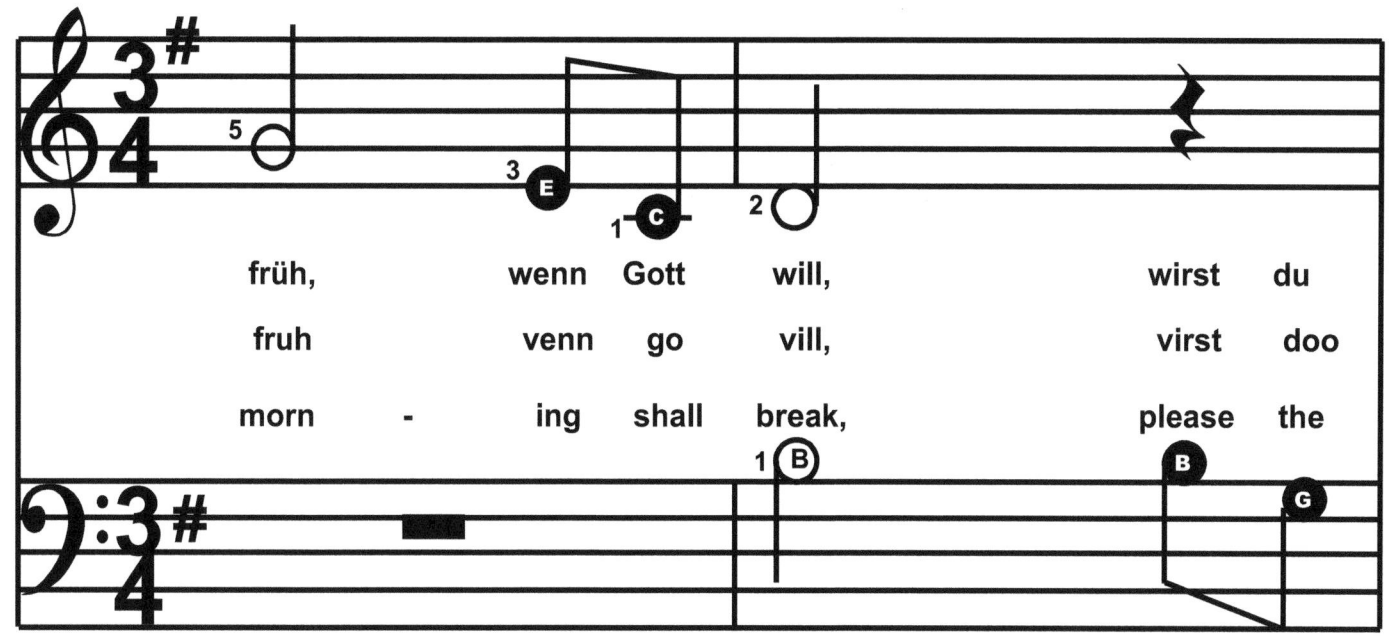

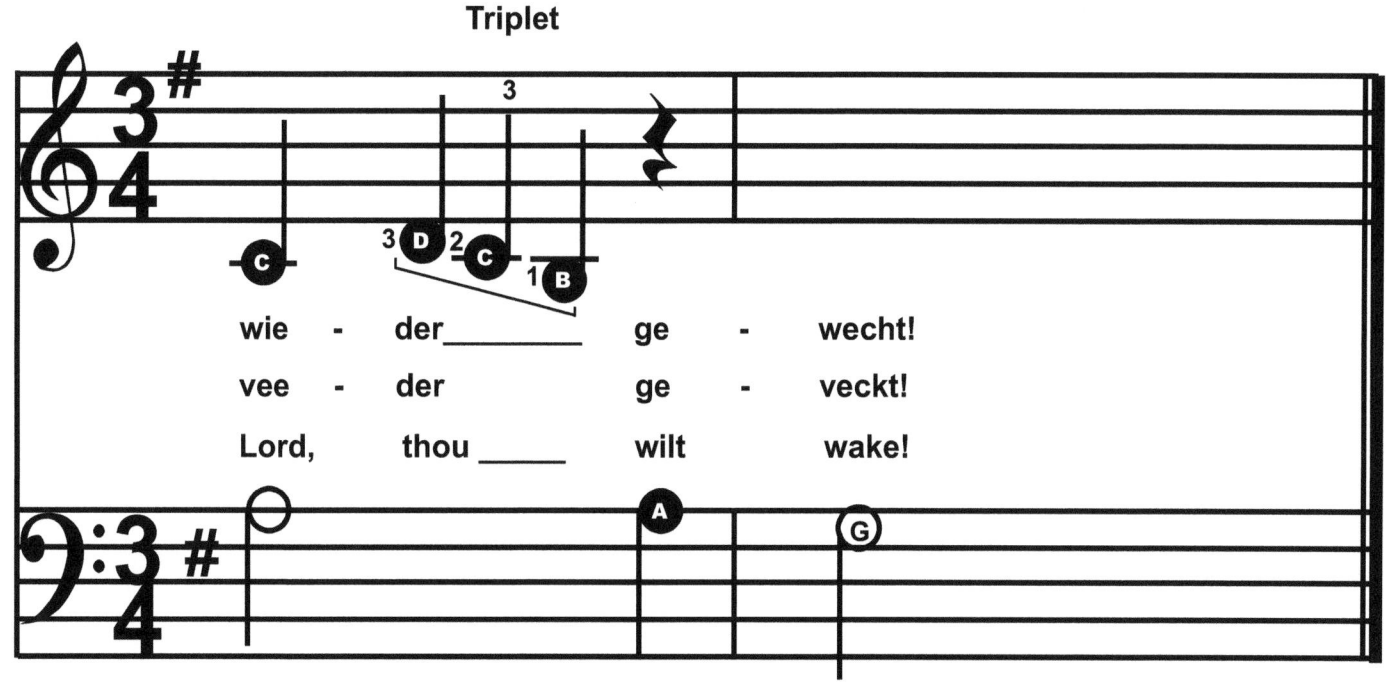

Triplet - When you see 3 notes grouped together as above you play all 3 notes evenly within the space of 1 count.

About The Author

Karol Ann Krakauer lives in Colorado with her husband, Michael Patritch. She is a retired Certified Nurse-midwife who has continued to play piano and pipe organ since childhood. She has been teaching piano since high school to friends and family. Her goddaughter asked her to teach her four children piano. When the youngest child was 19 months old he decided it was time for him to have his lesson. He climbed onto the piano bench, pushed his brother off and looked to Karol Ann to give him his lesson. She started with the dog house, aka the two black notes, and made him the wooden doggie block to put in the dog house. Next she made him a grandma block with his grandma's photo on it to place in grandma's house, aka the three black notes and so on. The rest as they say is history.

photo by Nancy Langstaff Krakauer

Thanks to Michael Patritch excellant editing assistance. Thanks also to my publisher, Aimee Fuhrman, for much support and knowledgeable input.

www.ingramcontent.com/pod-product-compliance
Lightning Source LLC
Chambersburg PA
CBHW042011150426
43195CB00002B/88